C000220083

CONTROLLED BURN

CONTROLLED BURN

How to Intentionally Set Fire to Your Life & Find the Living Hidden Beneath

Jeremy Fiebig

Jeremy Fiebig

Copyright © 2023 by Jeremy Fiebig

All rights reserved. No part of this book may be reproduced in any manner whatsoever without written permission except in the case of brief quotations embodied in critical articles and reviews.

First Printing, 2023

CONTENTS █

CONTENTS

This book is dedicated to my wife, Nan, and children; my daughter, Elliott, and son, Owen. Visiting state parks like Carver's Creek is one of our things.

ACKNOWLEDGEMENTS

I owe great thanks to all the professors in the Master of Arts in Liberal Studies program at UNC-Wilmington, to Heiwa no Bushi, Rev. Jeff Thornberg, and many others who gave me nothing but grace over the last few years.

I am grateful to the Arts Council of Fayetteville and Cumberland County, especially its grants staff including Sarah and Michael, for making the publication of this book possible. I also thank Shannon Camlin Ward, Beth Hess, Adrienne Trego, Veronica Colon, Paul Woolverton, Deborah Happel, Deb Streusand, Yolanda "Yogii" Barnes, Jessica Johnson, Jacob French, Scot McCosh, and many others.

This project is supported by a Mini Grant from the Arts Council of Fayetteville|Cumberland County in part by contributions from community partners, and through grants from the City of Fayetteville, Cumberland County, and the N.C. Arts Council, a division of the Department of Natural & Cultural Resources.

I thank Ralph Alan Cohen, who introduced me to St. Bartholomew's and to a host of other magical places in London and in the mystical Shenandoah Valley.

Lastly, I honor the work of my friends and colleagues at Sweet Tea Shakespeare as well as an anonymous personal assistant, whose work enabled me to create the boundaries of time and focus that enabled me to do this work on a busy and generally overcommitted schedule.

Preface

Controlled Burn

"The fires of sufferings become the light of consciousness." – Eckhart Tolle

I'm one of those people who stands around fires and whom everyone calls a pyromaniac. I am not a pyromaniac, I should note, but I am fascinated and mystified by the process of starting a fire. I should also note I'm a self-trained Midwesterner who sort of stacks the wood only a little neatly and doesn't mind cheating with some squirts of lighter fluid. I want to see that fire roar. I want to singe my finger hairs but not my facial hairs. I want to burn shit in that fire. I want to see old scripts I've printed burn. I want to see tin cans melt. I want to make lava. I want to eat a toasted marshmallow. I do not want to get cute with the s'mores recipe – the ritual and the simplicity of nostalgia do quite enough for me.

I've been around enough fires to know there are other people like me, the pseudo-pyromaniacs who also want to burn stuff. These people are useful and necessary. Party planners plan on having them, I promise you. The fire has to get started. It and the pyros are cheap entertainment. The fire entertains for a while and then the pyros take over. At first it's the easy stuff, the sticks and split wood. But then a scavenger hunt begins, all over the campsite or the yard or the house, pyros looking for the cool stuff to burn. Old dolls. Coke cans. Coke bottles, if you're lucky. Things that'll cause little pops and fizzes, but not explosions. Later in the party, when the flames are down and the embers are glowing hot, the shit to burn burns slowly. Those things are the main feature at this point, esthetically speaking.

Attendees in camp chairs, beers in hand, watch the slowly dissolving tin cans or whatever-it-is, enthralled. A strange thing happens at this time. The bodies of these humans at this fire are warm and lit on one side, cool and dark on the other, satellites drawn in by the gravity of this thing. The bodies are maybe buzzed or drunk. The bodies are full and fed. The dancing fire is doing its hypnotic work. The bodies are activated and safe, satisfied and occupied. And then the people show up. Their minds and hearts. Their selves. Their stories. Stories and Selves are capitalized here, primary in all senses of that word. The heat of excitement and celebration has slipped into the glow of this new, diaphanous thing. Reality is gauzy here, permeable. Shakespeare, speaking about something similar to this moment, refers to what it is: an insubstantial pageant.

Though I'll get to talking about bonfires, what I really want to do is help you light your own. This book is a mess of stuff aimed at helping you do just that. I start by talking about other manners of fire – cautionary tales, perhaps, about how to prevent forest fires and burnout and housefires and all of that. I follow the old logic that in order to understand a thing, it's helpful to understand what it isn't. It is about this approach that I need to beg your forgiveness before you go further. You see, I am an expert at bonfires – at least the metaphorical kinds I'll come to discuss. I am not an expert at the other kinds of figurative fires, even though I have experience with them, sometimes long, deep, hot experiences. This begins as a story – a drama – about fires, in which I am the thing that is on fire. Therefore, it is a drama about trauma. And for that reason, I probably have no business writing it. I am not a therapist. I am not a psychologist. I am barely a body expert. There is likely very little I have to say that is new or even terribly insightful about trauma or the ventures into recovery I'll mention. Even my central image – fire – is not new. Phoenixes have risen from ashes for quite some time. What's more, if I'm fuel for the bonfires I'll describe later on,

I'm still burning. But here we are. We might as well grab a beer and cook some hotdogs.

After we talk about these other kinds of fire, I've got a series of firestarters I'll share with you – projects, essays, reflections, and other sundries that may help you thin out the ground a bit and make space for a fire of your own. These endeavors are mostly disconnected from any grand narrative you might encounter, but my hope is that they'll prompt you in some artistic or poetical or embodied way to set your life on fire in a good way. These things worked for me to one degree or another. My thought is less that they will work for you and more that they might prompt something in you. Kindling, if you will.

Once these firestarters have done their work, I invite you to light some of your own fires. Perhaps it's a tad ambitious, but all fires have ambitions.

I've even included for you some pages to burn. Scribble in them. Journal. Respond to a couple of questions I've written for you. Tear them out and start your own fire – literal or figurative. The experience of doing so could become a bonfire experience, too.

Part 1

Catching Fires

Bonfires, Controlled Burns, and What They Make

Bonfires

This is a book about bonfires. All kinds. Big ones. Hot ones. Ones meant to burn dried-up things, whose sparks risk drifting too far on unpredictable breezes. Bonfires are dangerous. Bonfires scar the land. Generations from now – maybe even millennia – beings may stumble upon our campsites and our backyards and pick over black bits of wood and bone, charred tin cans, and other evidence of moments that we've chosen to burn. Bonfires pollute like tiny, acrid factories, pushing carbon and carcinogens into the air to be breathed in by trees and animals. Bonfires necessarily cause stories to happen where folks are gathered. Between and among those stories, in the dancing, orange light, in the danger, magic happens. Bonfires are things around which people gather, mesmerized by the flames, to share stories or meals or not to share at all. Bonfires are reflective spaces – thin spaces, I'll call them later – where we can sit and watch and think. And not think. Bonfires are meditative spaces. Dancing places. They meet some of the basic human needs in Abraham Maslow's hierarchy,[1] and they call forth the human practices of community and ritual from before the time of the Biblical Abraham. Light. Warmth. Belonging. Practice.

It's sometimes my job as a theatre person to hit others over the head with metaphor. I'm going to do that. It's also often my job as a professor and theatre director to stand in front of groups of people and ask, "Does that make sense?" I do this handfuls of times an hour if I'm lecturing. Now that I'm writing a book, the worst (or best – I'm a recovering pessimist) of these habits must come to bear. And so today we're going to talk about metaphorical bonfires, and I'm going to hope it makes sense and ever doubt that it does.

I am a storyteller by trade, and as I reflect on bonfires in this book, I see a common thread and set of themes weaving among and between the disparate, (too) narrowly specific stories I've chosen to tell: a call to engage in deep work, the work under the work. For example, I now find the depth of Jung in simple fairy tales[2], the purity of which embodies more in a page than an entire philosophical essay. That call for reflection, depth, and connection — story — resonates in me now in such a way that my work here is an examination of those vibrations and an opportunity to tell stories rich and vibrant in nature. I can think back to these few stories I'll share, some of them painful and confusing at the time, and view them through the lens of a gracious storyteller, closely examining the stumbles and pitfalls I've committed along the way as part of a larger journey. The work here affords me the chance to evaluate the present: my present, my state of recovery, and my emerging Self with a capital S.

Why Fires?

At several points in the writing process for this book, a collaborator would turn to me and ask "who are you writing for?" or "what do you hope to accomplish with this book?" or "what do you hope people will take away from this?" I have to admit I bristled at every one of these kinds of questions. Almost immediately each time, my mind went blank. Despite being a (very poorly self-taught) marketer, a teacher versed in things like learning outcomes, an actor taught to pursue objectives, and despite knowing that the idea of publishing a book is to sell it to people who will read it, I just don't know, y'all. On one hand, I'm afraid of telling these stories at all. I fear doing so is narcissistic, egotistical, vain, crude, or a sign of selling out. On the other hand, despite having benefited from some of them, self-help books and the self-help industry as a whole sometimes register with me as opportunistic and hollow – jobs for people who can't get real jobs. Or weirdos. On a third, mutant hand, the graced one that reminds me I am a freak in my own way, I think the point of such things – whether they be books like this or plays I direct or songs I sing or my classes when they are good – is to just light the way forward a little ways down the path. I may not be qualified as a lantern carrier. That's okay. I am on fire, after all. No expertise needed, just experience. I hope my experience helps you.

Fire is a thing to be loved. Being on fire, metaphorically speaking, can be quite all right, too. We all need a sense of community, something to gather around and feel safe in. We also need to feel risk, heat, drive, and the kind of dancing that fire does. This is especially true when the darkness closes in, when the cold sets in, or when we feel threatened by predators. A bonfire is a great place for this – it provides light and warmth, helping us to see and feel safe, and it is a place of some risk and play. It also helps us to get rid of underbrush, making it easier for us to see what's ahead and to grow new things. However, if left uncontrolled, fire can be dangerous and destructive. It can consume everything in its path and pose a threat to our safety. Therefore, it's important that we keep our environments clear and unburned, or they will quickly become out of control. Dead underbrush is dangerous, slippery, and yearning to burn. It's too "thick" - like the places we'll visit later.

Controlled Burning

A controlled burn is sometimes called a prescribed burn.[3] I love that word "prescribed" because it means planned. I think you'll find some prescriptions of the medical, chemical, and physical kinds are necessary for the ailments of the thing ablaze. In nature, controlled burns are scheduled for times when they don't pose a threat to people or property. This allows us to avoid the out-of-control burn that destroys everything in its path. By thinning the space intentionally, we are clearing out the overgrowth, the dead, and anything else that is no longer serving a purpose. This can be helpful in our personal lives as well, by creating these "thin spots" we can clear out the things that are no longer helpful or beneficial. Old cans. And can'ts.

This book is both a kind of controlled burn and a bit of a prescription for controlled burning that I hope will help you build your next fire. How big a fire is required? What are the environmental conditions needed to keep things safe and to promote new growth? How do we recognize when we're losing control of the fire? How do we manage the smoke? What protective equipment and methods do we need on hand? Maybe most importantly: who are we inviting to the bonfire and what should they bring?

One of the things I know to be true about me – and that Controlled Burning has cleared away and revealed – is that I'm what they used to call a Renaissance person. I think Renaissance person is often meant in the "jack of all trades" sense, not in the literal "rebirth" sense, but I'm taking on the mantle of both meanings. I mention this for two reasons. First, I'm going to hop all over the place with examples from really different places. Sometimes I'll make the effort to weave all those disparate instances together, but sometimes that's on you to sort out. You're different from me and that's a good thing. The core of my stuff will not be the same as yours, but the *process* of Controlled Burning can help get you to where you are going anyway. The second reason is that, like a good jack of all trades, I am master of very few. My examples will be limited to a few things I know fairly well, like stories, theatre, other rituals, events, environmental design, teaching or taking classes, and to several things about which I know much less, like architecture, theology, meditative practices, and various religious traditions – all metaphorical bonfires or potential ones. You do not have to be an expert in lighting or keeping fires to host a metaphorical barbecue in your backyard. But it's helpful if you're an expert at tending to the kinds of big bonfires that can ignite serious work in your life and community. And it is particularly important that you know what fuel sources you have at hand and how they burn. And what the fire gives birth to.

A Quick Note

One important thing I want you to know before reading further is that this is not a religious book. It does talk about religion – one of those trades of which I am a sometime jack – and a big church building, as well as Buddhism, and Baptists, among other things. I'll touch on religious themes and language and images and places from time to time across a wide spectrum of practices, and those come with whatever apologies are necessary for you to keep reading. But I'm not here to convert you. This is not a Christian Trojan Horse of a thing. No one will be busting out a guitar to sing worship choruses around our metaphorical bonfires. And so, what follows is for everyone. Or at least it is for you if it is for you.

The Work of Bonfires

This is a story about lighting and warming spaces and journeys –
what I'll call *Deep Work*. Deep Work is about designing the bonfire
experience, moving from raging risk and danger to a controlled
burn. About moving from personal crisis to self-renewal. To help
do your own Deep Work, you'll encounter the tools I used to start
and control the fire within myself, from therapy and spirituality to
self-care and study. I say "encounter" the tools because I'm going
to mention them in my context but will not teach you to use them
in yours.

Deep Work and The Work and Controlled Burning, which I'll
sometimes use interchangeably, are phrases used in a lot of those self-
help books I sometimes loathe and sometimes love and sometimes
use as fuel for fires, literal and figurative. You'll witness some of the
discoveries I've made in the light of these fires, from the importance
of connecting the elements with my core identity to learning to
release some core elements, too.

A fire creates and destroys. We tend to think of creation as a good
thing and destruction as a bad thing, but I'm here to tell you that the
creation of a raging forest fire that burns homes and lives is no good.
And the destruction of the effects of trauma is very good. We have to
take care both with what we create and what we clear and burn.

Deep Work often finds us by way of simple themes: creation, destruction, story, fairy tale, nature, space. I'll look a bit at all of these
themes. If you find my stories too indirect, too abstract, I invite you
back here to refresh yourself on how they connect.

The Work is often buried under what we call "work" – that's why
we have to get to thin places and do a controlled burn of the "work"
that distracts us to see what's really underneath. Also, the work we

think we're doing is almost never the work we're actually doing, but is instead an honorable but naive efforts at recovery or self-care or manifestation or pick-your-self-help-buzz-word. These efforts often don't light the spark or that might pour unnecessary fuel on a very hot fire.

Instead, Deep Work is spending time in the darkness – the tomb – working the ground, laying out the kindling, planning for the as-yet-unrealized hope that this space and ourselves and our communities will soon find light and warmth.

The Work is the story – the reflection, the depth, the yearning for connection – we will tell around the bonfire. The ones that are true and truly us, not the ones we distract ourselves with. Not the ones we want others to tell about us.

The Work is becoming a gracious storyteller – embracing the singed whiskers and the drunken honesty and the friends who didn't accept the invitation – not glossing over the stumbles and pitfalls, but embracing them as inevitable and welcome in the story.

Controlled Burning is deconstruction – the preparation for and execution of the controlled burn when we are intentional and the uncontrolled blaze when we are not – the burning of no longer useful things, harmful fuels, risky environments.

Deep Work is party planning. The bonfire begets community. Meals. Bread and wine and marshmallow communions. Laughter. Belonging. Shared Stories.

The Work is intentionally setting things on fire and letting them burn and burn. It is also not letting things catch fire unintentionally or, if they do, finding a way to use the fire for good destruction and not bad destruction.

Controlled Burning is tending to the fire and the things on fire. At the end of the bonfire and the end of our journeys, we emerge new and transformed. The thin space thickens, the night of enthralling wonder and sparks and stars slips off into dreams and slumber. But someone has to put out the fire or make sure it goes out on its own. Someone has to awaken and tend to the forest and the char.

Deep Work is reconstruction. It is taking delight in new things. It is hope that the forest will see new sprigs of green – tender, weak, but delightful in their hopefulness. A sign of new life. It is walking around covered in beautiful soot.

Overall, Controlled Burning is an invitation to be active and experiential in The Work – not simply watching the fire happen, but tending to it, making space for it, and inviting folks over to share in it. Reading this book but never going into the woods for yourself (both literally and figuratively) will do you little good.

Let's light a fire, gather 'round, and tell stories.

Definitions

I've introduced some terms here and will bring some others to bear before too long. Let's take a moment to define them. Definition – as in where the fire can and cannot go – is one of the hallmarks of Controlled Burning.

- *Body*: Our own bodies, the bodies of our communities (i.e., a theatre company or a religious body or even a great class), and the bodies of the things we make, including bonfires.
- *Bonfire*: The actual thing burning. Could be oneself (metaphorically speaking, of course), a campfire, or an event, moment, or season of time. Sometimes I use this image interchangeably as a concrete or embodied emblem for Controlled Burning.
- *Bonfire Experience*: A magical series of moments that happen when the space in our lives thins out, our senses and stories take over, and transformation happens. A Bonfire Experience can involve a literal bonfire or a metaphorical or symbolic one. A good play is a Bonfire Experience. A great meal, like a potluck, held in community, can be a Bonfire Experience. There are tons of other examples. Managed well, a Bonfire Experience can be sustained throughout one's life as an individual and as a community.
- *Controlled Burning*: the ongoing, necessary, destructive-and-creative work that is essential to bring about new growth – and the personal, communal, or ecological art of burning the (metaphorical) undergrowth in the thick places in our lives. Sometimes used interchangeably with Deep Work or The Work.

- *Deep Work*: The Work under the work that makes the magic happen: using the fire intentionally and well. Sometimes used interchangeably with Controlled Burning.
- *Embodied*: The quality of being in the body – one's own, a corporate one, or a physical object like a piece of art.
- *Magic*: The moments of ineffable, ethereal, and often indescribable transformation that happen in all kinds of bodies as a result of Controlled Burning, Bonfire Experiences, and The Work.
- *The Work*: See Deep Work.
- *Thick*: The nature of detritus around us – literal and metaphorical, physical, mental, spiritual, and relational – that has caught or easily catches fire.
- *Thin*: The quality of space, time, and spirit that is clear of thickness, eager for possibility, and ready for magic to happen.

Uncontrolled Burning

Turning Big Burns into Bonfires

The Other Kinds of Fire

In order to talk about bonfires, I want to talk about other kinds of fires that are sometimes not so good: housefires, wildfires, and self-immolation. Not that many years ago, I was on fire, and not in a good way. A part of me was burnt out for sure, and the rest of me – and nearly everything around me, it seemed – was flaming out in a hurry. The alarms of Crisis were sounding. That crisis, I have come to learn, was a deep, months-and years-long trauma response to elements of my professional and personal life that I hadn't tended to properly in a long time, if ever. I had not cleared the proverbial underbrush. I had not prevented forest fires. My fire, like all the infamous forest fires we hear about these days, risked making the headlines.

This particular fire started like a lot of fires do. I'm an ambitious and privileged and energetic guy. I'm a tenured Professor of Theatre and Directing and spent most of my professional life aiming to achieve exactly what I'd achieved, but it came at a high cost. I didn't take care of myself in almost every sense of that notion, and my work environments, particularly at my teaching institution and in a theatre company I founded, were not nurturing either. There were big and little traumas that had been building throughout my entire journey, and they erupted all at once and messily.

Once you're flaming out, there is only so much you can do. Sometimes you just have to watch yourself burn.

I mentioned earlier I'm one of those pseudo pyromaniacs who likes burning stuff in bonfires. While I'm not an actual pyromaniac, I have been a metaphorical one. While I've always been on fire in some way, in the span of not that many years, I added on a lot of fuel – not just to see how it would burn, but burning it more or less because I could. I burned things by:

- obtaining two master's degrees in Shakespeare,
- earning my first tenure-track job,
- finding a new tenure-track job during the immediate aftermath of the 2008 housing and economic crisis that caused my first institution to be threatened with closure,
- becoming a parent of two children,
- climbing a second tenure mountain,
- founding a theatre company,
- producing or directing or designing or acting in, like, a bajillion plays and musicals,
- obtaining promotion to full professor status early.

In burning these things (and several others), parts of myself and my life I didn't want to catch fire had done so. The realization was slow to come.

People smarter than me will read all this and wisely suggest that I had not been engaging in something like self care. This is true. I had not taken much chance to feed myself in any deep, human sense. I was a feeder—a teacher, a founder, a director, a parent—but was not being fed. In ways that have now become the American and

Western cliché, I climbed the mountain(s), looked around, and said, collapsing in a fit of burnout, "this is it?"

I think self-care is a bit of a trite response to this kind of stuff happening in on-fire people whose heart is in the right place, as I think mine mostly was. I saw – and see – my energy, my on-fire-ness, as a gift. That's fair. Wanting to create magic as an artist is a kind of flame that is put out too often by parents and grandparents who'd prefer you'd be an accountant, thank you very much. Wanting to take advantage of my own energy and privilege was a good thing. And it had worked, not only by a measure of my own accomplishments, but in communities I'd formed and stories I'd been a part of telling. These are good things. And I would not be where I am – and the good fires I've lit would not still be burning – if I'd worked much differently. In the story of things, sometimes stuff will catch fire when you're playing with it, especially when you're younger (and stupider). That's not necessarily allowed, but it does happen. As does all shit. That said, we want bonfires, not five-alarm blazes – especially those that risk hurting other people. There is a kind of care needed, a kind of fire prevention. That's partly why I'm writing this book. We have to tend the fires and the ecosystem, ourselves, our fuels, and the other metaphorical pyromaniacs in our lives.

A bit more on these other metaphorical pyros: watch out. Your fire(s) may be under some kind of control, but then some doofus shows up with a tank of gasoline and some bottle rockets. They should know better, but often they don't. And when you both don't know better, yikes. Things will flame up, and there will be almost nothing you can do until you're forced to do something big, dramatic, and drastic. This shit also happens.

Anyway, there I am. Life on fire. All parts. Things I've built are burning like crazy. Relationships torched. Burned out on work. Burned out on stuff I used to love. Fried. It *does* matter how I got there, don't get me wrong. For now, though, let's return to that image of a person and the spaces they belong to, for good reasons and bad ones, collapsed from burning too hot for too long. Some of you have been there.

Deconstruction

"Nature will create its own fires to keep the ecosystem in check," my therapist recently told me. When I mentioned I was writing this thing, they slid that in with a wink, along with the fact that they'd worked for the Georgia Forestry Service in college. I've come to learn that this process – creating fires to keep things in check – when applied to people, has a name: deconstruction. I use the term in its popular sense, though one that nonetheless leans on the work of Jacques Derrida and others who developed the philosophy. Deconstruction is a realization of meaninglessness. One builds something —for years, decades even—and then dies. Civic institutions erode. Language fails. The American dream doesn't work. Deconstruction is what happens when the illusions underpinning our thoughts, worldview, and ways of being are exposed. It is the compelled dismantling of systems, assumptions, habits, and beliefs that, though they once were all that mattered, do not matter anymore.

There are different kinds of deconstruction. Some can be handled mindfully, like a conscientious divorce, or a spiritual awakening, or what happens when one's child is born, and everything takes on different meaning.

Trauma is what happens, I think, when people and their bodies, beliefs, and relationships are deconstructed without their knowledge or consent. Trauma, despite the intensity of the pain, is experienced as a passive process. Trauma is not Descartes sitting in his easy chair contemplating what he knows and cannot know. Trauma is turning to a trusted friend of twenty years during a time of personal need, and having the friend walk away. It's no longer understanding how the world works, how people work, and literally not even knowing what is real. Even if the deconstruction is happening within oneself, it is as though one's mind and body have another self actively dismantling them from the inside. The house of cards that was one's life collapses, and the resulting despondence is as permeating as death. There is no comfort even, from one's faith, since those core beliefs are usually traumatically deconstructed as well.

Much of what I outline here was an attempt to control an ongoing and out of control period of deconstruction in my life. To control the wildfire. But as I meditated, I came to realize that life is anything but control. Life is akin to a kind of death, an experience of being completely out of control. My prior decade of pursuing tenure and promotion, teaching, leading productions at my home institution, engaging in a side acting, directing, and theatre management career in the region, and founding and operating a theatre company had caused all control to disappear.

I thought that in most respects, the deconstruction had already happened, and I was nowhere to be found. Whatever had been me, whatever self was forming in prior decades, became a composition of tasks and achievements, bit parts in other people's work. This is not uncommon, I think, particularly among men, who are taught to build things at the behest of others, on their own and especially outside of their families. Many men wake up, as I did, in the middle of a midlife crisis, wondering why they suddenly don't understand the world around them, even though they built it. That was certainly part of my story.

In just about every way one can imagine, I had dissolved. Because of teaching and theatre obligations, it was common for me not to see my wife and kids for more than maybe an hour a day, usually while

I was bleary eyed and one of us was on the way to something else. My schedule pulled me far out of physical health as I dieted on fast food and quick buffets during a day that began with work early in the morning and ended with work late at night. Even vacations were invaded with long phone calls and long sessions when I was hunched intently over a laptop. I experienced acute anxiety, not merely about the endless work list, but by my absolute obsession over it.

I visited therapists off and on with no real solution available in traditional talk therapy. At work, I encountered a toxic environment on a daily basis, regular bullying, and persistent questioning of my interests and abilities. In an early attempt to escape the toxicity and lack of collegiality, I'd taken up a longtime dream of founding a theatre company in what was, then, spare time. The theatre company became the place where I exercised my best self, tried to escape toxicity by creating a community free of it, and where I could make close, creative, collaborative friendships. That worked for a while, but as it grew—and I wanted it to grow—it became my Adam, a new body of work I became obsessed over, and a monster beyond my control. Both at work and at the theatre company, I felt myself entirely consumed, invisible, almost as though I had facilitated excellence and community in those spaces but never fully took part in them.

As these things consumed me to the point of annihilation, I found other familiar interests. I took up a craft beer obsession for a while. I plugged in more fully at my church as a quasi-staff member, something that felt comforting in part because I'd grown up in church. I joined committees and boards and commissions, telling myself I owed it to the communities to which I belonged (and that it helped my tenure portfolio). As my life became more out of balance, all my noble efforts devolved into work, tasks, and resentment. And all of the work reinforced the idea that it (my work) and not me (my true Self) were the reasons I had any worth at all. To counter the building resentment, feelings of invisibility and being overwhelmed, I passed the work off to others in a series of co-dependent relationships and arrangements where I made other people necessary for my success and happiness, and not in a good way.

While I was over-committed everywhere and consumed by everything, in no place was the lack of boundaries more apparent, and in no place was a turbulent deconstruction taking place more than in the theatre company. What had been created as a sanctuary became a business. No longer was I a magician cultivating magic in the hearts and minds of artists and audience, but instead I was an owner, a boss, and an alien. At the highest pitch of the resounding crisis of self was a crisis at the theatre company. Just as I'd allowed myself to become unhealthy, my unhealthy behavior toxified that place. And every place else, too. Home. Church. Work. But especially the theatre company. I'm noting this for reasons that will become apparent later: theatre can be a kind of bonfire. It isn't meant to be a wildfire. That is true of a lot of communities and places of belonging.

Death

Housefire, wildfire: this was my story a few years ago. And as the fires burned most of me up, somewhere – deep inside – I recognized, on a bodily level more than an analytic one, that I was in deconstruction. At first, it was all panic. I set off every alarm imaginable. I screamed – literally, quite often into my pillow and my windshield and also in the sense that every communication I had with other people was me screaming for something. Help, if nothing else. I cried and mourned. The panic manifested in my body, for the first time in its history, waking up at 4am, alert, on fire, and ready to move. Rather than fight the insomnia, I started walking, obsessively, until at least some of the energy burned off, for miles and hours around the college campus near where I lived. Miles and miles around the track. I screamed there, too, silently at the fires there with me: Jupiter, Saturn, and Uranus breaking over the line of longleaf pines which themselves caught fire as the sun came up. That sounds poetic, maybe, but I've come to learn it was a flight response, a huge one, to what I was experiencing as a trauma engulfing every splinter of my life.

Before and after and in between episodes of these flight responses, I was fighting too. I am a fighter in the sense that I'm a natural born contrarian and am in the ninety-ninth percentile for world's worst cases of Resting Bitch Face. I also have a knack for annihilation. At the time, I suppose I thought that if I'm burning, the world might as well. I fought myself. Of course not all of this fighting was good. I lost a lot and so did other people around me and I don't want to minimize that. I can mourn some of the effects of the uncontrolled burn and be grateful that some of the stuff needed to go and did.

Throughout my time as a makeshift trauma first responder, this brand of self-taught, homemade fire fighting had me scrambling through a host of attempts at stabilization, triage, and control. I started working out. I started a diet and lost seventy pounds (not including that thirty of those pounds I lost twice). I went back to therapy. I engaged in spiritual studies. I joined a weird graduate program. I meditated. I medicated. I made plays. I listened closely to what my wife and kids said about me, and started to believe it. I called my folks to tell them what was up. I said honest things to people I loved and respected. I started to set up boundaries for the first time in living memory – fire lines, let's call them, ways of letting the uncontrolled fires burn to a reasonable point. I'd describe these attempts as the difference between allowing the house to burn up and collapse, condemned and dangerous, versus wielding the duties of demolition to an intentional, careful, and relational process. Wildfire versus controlled burn. You get it.

At the beginning and in the middle and at the end of this fight and flight stuff – hell, even now, as I look back on it with some perspective – I was not any good at it on my own. I needed professionals, trained folks who knew what they were doing, to tell me "First, you have to stop adding fuel to the fire, you dope. Then, you have to start to suppress it." I watched a television show lately with a huge fire that engulfed the entire wing of a castle. There were professional firefighters depicted on those long, extendable ladders, with a huge spray of water. The fire doesn't do anything. It roars larger for a long time. Professionals know this and spray the spray anyway. Because they also know that you give everything a good soak, eventually the fuel is no good. Here I was burning and raging but The Work was working, too. The fire would only spread so far, even though it might take a good long time to burn out, if it ever did.

You may be intuiting a good bit about intention here. While I think it's probably true that if you don't intend the fires to keep raging, you've begun to get them under control in the sense that *only you can prevent forest fires.* It is also true that the road to very fiery places is paved with the best of intentions. For me, intention works best when it informs action: when I breathe, move, work, and speak with intention. I also have to say it's helpful if you're right – if the intention and the work you're doing with it is right. Even this good intention may not be enough. When my dark night of the soul was at its darkest several years ago, I remember telling my therapist that nine out of ten days were awful. That was probably me being optimistic. The thing is, I *intended* to come out of this season of deconstruction every second I was awake (and plenty of moments when I was dreaming, I now know). Intention is an unlit match, a bottle of lighter fluid, and some wood. The Work is making those things talk to each other. Controlled Burning – in the sense of the body and mind here – is a metabolic process, the fire that burns both requires and consumes energy in one's body. Controlled Burning deals with the trauma by using it as fuel; transformation is the name of the game.

At several points earlier in my journey, I would have sworn that if only I could more actively or *intentionally* engage in the process of deconstruction, it would no longer be "trauma." Gosh, was I wrong about that. The thing is, so long as the fires are burning, you are always in the process of *recovering* what you can, and never in the process of being *recovered*. And even when you think you're recovered, bits of you will always be charred at the edges, stained with soot, and even wrinkled up in the waters of recovery. The smell of smoke will linger. The thing about deconstruction is that even if you are going to dismantle the place, it is best to save the photo albums and your favorite blanket: the meanings you want to retain in terms of defining who you are. So I tried to sort through that which could be saved, versus that which must be let go. This is a kind of Controlled Burning, too: deciding what you will allow to be burned, and that which you'll save from the fire.

Deconstruction, if one survives it, invites reconstruction. The timber of the shipwreck builds new rafts and leads to the promise of new life and new meaning informed by the artifacts of the past. While recovering, I encountered new frameworks and ideas that enabled me to start stitching meaning back together. I uncovered the power of meditation for a while and ultimately, the importance of daily habit and ritual in my life. I found new communities and friendships. I started following a Buddhist teacher. I found an Episcopal priest who was comfortable enough with me to tell me the real deal. I learned about panentheism as a counter balance to the Western emphasis on dualism, the maxim that all is either God or not

God. Instead, panentheism offers a way of considering ourselves as connected with each and every other life on earth, all imbued with a kind of holiness and grace that is actively trying to save itself from its own trauma. After growing up as the son of a Baptist pastor and schoolteacher, (the product of theatre people and church people), I'd awakened to the notion that everything is a performance if the ego is involved, and everything is real if it is not.

Particularly useful for me at this time was reading Jeffrey Kripal's exploration of the "cosmic humanities." In his work, Kripal explores ways of thinking about and believing in a cosmos of interconnected reality, "transmigration of memory and personality," and the idea that our work as humans (and humanists) is in these ever-erupting, richly unfolding waves of magic, wonder, and awe. Kripal also points us to the notion of "mutants" as subjects and agents of transformation, Christological figures, shamans; people of real magic are the bodies where such wonders take place. Reconstruction is the work of such magicians and mutants. Reconstruction is this very mutation, the common thread pointing us toward the cosmic human story, awakenings, mutations, and the possibility of magical transformation—of and in the bodies of the self and of the community. Simply put, if we are burning, burnt, or about to be burned, we are subjects of transformation.

Amid the rubble of my personal deconstruction, the remnants that began to emerge for me were new understandings of what is important in life and a new belief in the possibility of hope. I realize I am describing a process of learning. But there is a type of learning that is merely constructive, building credits towards a predetermined goal, and a type of learning that is experiential and ultimately transformative as one becomes something new. My job as a teacher of undergraduates and a director of actors is to gently and conscientiously help students observe what *they* may wish to deconstruct about themselves – so they may tear down the bad habits and social fears and poor techniques and establish stronger ways of working. It is also the work of therapy, the work of relationships, the work of the body, and the work of grace.

For me, then, this work (i.e., "The Work") represents time in the tomb, a kind of death—or at least a meditation on death. But death with new life is different from...terminal death, where the story ceases to continue.

It is also different from the death of a leg and learning to live as an amputee for the rest of one's life.

It is different even from heart surgery, whereby one continues to live, but with a new heart that came from another body, grown by another human.

Death is complete annihilation of the way the story of one's life has been told so far.

And before the story of my new life could emerge, I had to fully embrace the level of my prior *and on-going* annihilation. My mortal life. My living death.

Imagine being mindlessly trapped by all your worst habits for the better part of a decade. Now imagine that there are only two ways out: to drop them all, if you can, and recede into a cave of burnout and dissociation and resentment *or* engage in the uncomfortable and slow and tiresome work of undoing all those habits, one by one, and putting yourself back on a path to health. Then imagine having to do that second option in every area of your life. Every single one. Imagining shopping around for doctors and therapists until you can find some that are present enough with you to tell you what's going on. Imagine the loss of many good friends. Imagine finding new friends who won't let you do to them what you got away with before. Imagine telling your peers and colleagues and people who work for you your most intimate secrets. Imagine those secrets are diagnoses of the mind and body. Imagine seeking and finding real and impactful spiritual help, the wonders of new therapeutic techniques, and the magic of disciplined work on the mind and body. Some of you don't have to imagine.

Discovery

To the extent that there is a controlling idea or driving engine behind my work, it is to explore and embody my new insights from my journey back to health: to make what I've learned are Bonfire Experiences. I've found a welcome place to do that in art. Don't get me wrong: art isn't the *only* place where I've worked to create a Controlled Burn. There's also therapy, the gym, and a host of modalities we can talk about the next time we're at a campfire together. But I'm here to talk about art, in part, as a way out of the darkness, a rewiring and reworking and undoing of bad habits in the creation of new worlds. And while undoing my bad habits eventually led me back to examining and seeking joy and pleasure in art once again, I encountered the need to do so authentically. I could not simply reconstruct what pieces of my former life I had managed to save from the wreckage as some sort of spiritual collage. The annihilation I had experienced in my previous life needed to be replaced by a new kind of life-giving annihilation, the kind of which Buddhists' "death of ego" and Christ's "cross" represent.

Definition

Art is, in part, the creation of a body by a body for other bodies. Each of these kinds of bodies have slightly different, but sometimes overlapping, definitions. The easiest one is "by a body." That body is mine. Or yours. Whomever is making the thing. It's often an individual, but can be a collective body, too, like a choir or a theatre company or a band or a co-op of some sort. The "of a body" definition is what's being created. It is a thing – a painting, an event, a play, a sculpture, a process, or even a way of making. The "for other bodies" body is the audience, the stream of museum visitors, the readers, and these bodies could be a series of individuals or collective bodies taken as a whole – a church congregation, a sangha, a classroom, a whole institution. So a painter can make a painting for observers in a gallery. A choir can make a concert or an album for listeners. And so on. I mentioned there are overlaps, and this is where things get tricky. A theatre company can make itself for itself. Here, the body is making the body for the body, kind of like an individual might work out and diet and meditate and create to craft itself into a better version of itself. But I digress.

Bonfires are bodies – of wood, flame, air, and ember and their metaphorical counterparts – made by bodies (those who started the fire) to make new bodies – moments of connection, belonging, story, and transformation. They attract. They signal. They mesmerize and enchant. They clear space – both in how we prepare for them, thinning the ground they are meant for, and in that they burn up things and make them into thin air and ash. They glow, albeit briefly. They are here and then gone.

When I speak of bonfires, you have the image in your head. I want to overlay onto that image the metaphorical and personal and imaginative and communal bonfires I mean when I use the word. A great play is a bonfire. It is an empty space, filled with glowing, ephemeral things. It is a story. It is a communal experience. It is a ritual. It is a thing from which we leave transformed. All great art is a bonfire. Great parties are bonfires. Intentional design can be a bonfire. A person – electric, charismatic, and present – can be a bonfire. Bodies of all kinds – especially when they are used well –

are bonfires. In short, bonfires are anything where bonfire stuff happens: the space thins, the stories start, the magic happens, and where perfectly beautiful things burn and burn and burn, and where new beauty emerges.

Delight

This morning, on my way out of the store to buy some bonfire material, which in this case was some coffee concentrate, Vanilla Coke Zero, and coconut-almond coffee creamer – stuff that helps me burn through the afternoon fog – two things happened at the same time. A woman two cars down from me had her window open, a sometime-treat in North Carolina Decembers. This morning it was 63 degrees, overcast, and almost muggy. She was singing loudly along with some Gospel music that talked about how we've made it through. She was not a good singer, but she was into it, occasionally breaking from the song to wish everyone within hearing distance a good morning. Overhead, a Canada goose, also flying solo, honked its glottal blast. Together, this duet is fire. It is Spirit. It is good.

Burning changes things, and I left this moment this morning changed by this brief bonfire experience. The cliche, of course, is of the "refining fire," the one that burns away all the detritus and leaves something pure, pristine, and precious. This is not untrue, but it is also an incomplete understanding. Some fires just burn until whatever's in them is functionally gone – ash and soot and scar are all that remain. Some fires singe our finger hairs. In forestry, controlled burns kill all the dead stuff *and* the nascent growth on the forest floor, along with the vines creeping up the sides of trees. The point of some burns is just to make things disappear, to spend energy for its own sake. The point of a bonfire, then, is not to alter a product, but to create a moment where delight is possible. Or maybe several moments. Or a process. Or a season. Or, if we're careful stewards, a lifetime.

For a bonfire to be delightful, we have to steward it, to manage its intensity – just like we have to manage ourselves when we are the thing on fire. Sometimes the fire has to rage. Sometimes we must allow it to singe our whiskers – to be so close to us that it is not merely warm, but hot. To steward a bonfire is to also add fuel to it. This is massively counterintuitive in our age of self-care and in our perpetual concern about burnout. If we wish to keep our fires burning, the solution to burnout is to add the right fuel – fuel that excites the flames again and that allows us to return to the entrancing watch of the bonfire experience.

Fuel can be a lot of things, of course, and it's here I'll mention that the purpose of fuel is to burn. Trees can act as fuel for a fire, but their purpose is not to burn. The purpose of wood is not to burn – and some of it will not. The purpose of dead wood *might* be to burn, or it might be to build. The purpose of paper, (another dead tree product) might be to burn, or it might be to create or inspire. If you ask me, the marshmallow's purpose is to burn until charred on the outside and gooey on the inside. The marshmallow, made almost entirely of sugar, is a plant product, right alongside trees. It was once alive. It is now to be sacrificed to create a moment of delight.

Fuel can be almost anything, but the best stuff is the organic stuff of the earth, stuff that was once alive, (whose greenness has leached out over time and across the seasons,) chopped up, processed even, and thrown on the fire. In our metaphorical bonfires, in the moments and places and communities and art and expressions that give us life, we too have to burn up what was once alive, growing, and well. Sometimes we have to do so with the brush we've cleared out of our lives – the convenient stuff, the self-care stuff – and some-times we have to do it with what was once a beloved tree, whatever such a tree might be in our lives. In other words, our bodies have to burn. Other bodies have to burn. We can be our own fuel in this way. Our bodies have to sing with the songs coming through open windows and the honks in the December air. Our bodies have to burn on treadmills and on cushions and other places where we can burn ourselves up – but never out.

Bonfires burn up fuel so that they can create. In theatre, we call such things "strike." After a production closes, we intentionally dismantle everything we built for it that once created such life, such delight. We do this so that space for new life and light can be made. Strike is not an admission of defeat, but a hallmark of renewal: there is more to come, and we're making space for it.

Art and other kinds of expression can be fuel. Communities of belonging can also be fuel – both for the fire itself and for the experience around the fire.

Delight defines the bonfire experience. This is why a great party or an inspired organization are potentially amazing bonfire experiences. It is not merely about what's burning, but what's happening around the fire – the party, the gathering, the stories, the thinning out of Selves and the taking off of masks and the reality that emerges as the fire burns up the veils of vanity. The bonfire experience is itself a kind of art. There are the inviters, the party planners, the space makers, the pseudo pyromaniacs, the good storytellers, the professional extroverts who get things moving, the parents who have to get their kids to bed, the folks who show up late but with the really good beer, the late shifters, post-party arrivals who are, maybe, the only ones this whole thing is for.

The bonfire experience can even be for oneself as one occupies each of those roles over the course of a night or even the much longer Dark Night of the Soul. The bonfire is a community of ephemerality, of moments, of sparks and embers that might catch something else, even themselves, on fire.

Delight is not to be confused with pleasure. The delight of a thing emerges not merely from familiarity, but from the possibility of discomfort and difference. There is a delight in ritual, to be sure, in the laying of logs in familiar patterns and in a frequently used guest list. Even these rituals, however, prompt the possibility of activation, change, and transformation. The bonfire experience is not the slog of work and carpools. It is not a spreadsheet. It is the Thing that is not these things; the surprise, the risk of an errant but vital spark, the chance to learn, the new thing being created, even if the ground is familiar and the practice routine, like a cup of coffee or a quiet walk across the parking lot first thing this morning. Delight is both the journey into difference and the return from it.

The delight of the bonfire experience happens in the body – it is an embodied experience that stands outside the analytical, causal, linear, overly-planned ways we so often run our lives. That's in part why vacations, when we do them right, feel so delightful. New food, new scenery, new (if only brief) habits, new sounds, new smells. Bonfires are such experiences. For me, walking across the threshold of a playing space invites such an experience, as does making art, eating really good food, or creating community.

You'll notice I've gone out of my way to talk about bodies to this point. Bodies and bonfires are not a natural fit, poetically speaking (unless, perhaps, you're into Guy Fawkes or witches on stakes). What's more, I've waxed even more poetically than I am wont to do to try to make it work, veering into discussions about art and delight and trees and delight and communities and vacations and geese. Some of that poetry is necessary, but it may not be helpful. Here's the deal: what we're talking about when we talk about bonfires are experiences that happen in the body (however we've defined it to this point) that change the body. That change can be deconstruction. It can be death. It can be discovery. It can be delight. Bonfires, both literal and metaphorical, are environmental, creative, destructive experiences that transform how we make sense of the world.

How we make sense of the world comes from the thing that is doing the sensing. If nothing is making sense in your life, you have to change what you are sensing and what you are sensing with. In this way, The Work is body work, whether the body is our art, our communities, our experiences, our parties, our literal bonfires, or ourselves. Our bodies are the only ways we experience the bonfire – the warmth of the circle around it, the light of its dancing flames, the sound of its crackle and the stories around it, the taste of the food it cooks, the smell of its smoke. Bonfires delight us because of their difference from everything else we experience in our bodies. In this way, Controlled Burning – bonfire management – is a kind of environmental design we engineer so our bodies can engage in the full sensory experience.

The connection between bonfire, body, and Controlled Burn may be tenuous. It certainly isn't concrete. That is, perhaps, bound to happen when your writer is an abstract thinker, an organic creative for whom everything is both the right and wrong answer at the same time. I get that this stuff won't work for everyone. For some folks, a fire is just a hot, orange thing. For me, this connection, however loosely held together, is important for what lies ahead. The rest of this book is different – and hopefully in a delightful way – less like a singular, burning thing and more like the ephemeral stories unfolding around it. In that regard, the party's just getting started.

Design

Among my many trades as a Renaissance man is that of Designer – of spaces and experiences and what happens to bodies in them. I became good at this design stuff several years ago after a long stretch of not being good at it at all, and in this regard design is like a practice – and I had a lot of it. Most of my design work has been in theatre and event planning, where I try to take simple, elemental stuff – fabric, cafe lights, lanterns, a grass patch, music, some wood, some words, and a few good-hearted humans – and make something impactful, transformative, and magical. At home, my family will tell you, I design everything, collecting and curating objects and art, assembling these disparate pieces into some sort of cohesive whole alongside weird furniture, cool lighting, and what my friends call "drapey fabrics." These impulses carry over into my working and creative life as I design plays and the events around them, class sessions, curriculum, modest attempts at graphic design, occasional liturgies, concert playlists, and even the bumper stickers on the back of my truck. Doing all this design all the time is a major factor in what makes me good at it – I am always playing, always practicing, always creating. The work can benefit others. It can make communities. It can create a bonfire experience. As good as I am applying this kind of design out in the world, I have incredible trouble doing it in my own life, and so: a story – a design digression, if you will.

The shortest of beginnings: I lived for a long time in constant fear of being erased. I don't use that word lightly – I probably mean something more like annihilated. I've done a lot of therapy and a lot of work on why this might be the case, and I have only some answers. I think I was born sensitive and impressionable, as a lot of artists are. Sometime in childhood, I took in the message that what I do is more important than who I am. In junior high and high school, something like this was reinforced by relatively minor bullies and religion

– sometimes those things are the same thing – that *both* what I do and who I am were somehow wrong. By the time I got to college, I was burning hot – shining brightly on anger and the wrong kind of righteousness – a reaction to being snuffed out, dampened, and ignored. I worked ceaselessly. Over a span of years in high school, and college, and then again late in graduate school into my first job, I did not have more than two weeks off – and usually not more than a handful of days – between major productions. I lived in the theatre, whichever one it was, pulling easily twelve- to fifteen- hour days as a rule. I was proving myself – and proving that I existed. If design is me making a mark – insisting that I have an impact on the world and, in not a small number of cases, requiring the audience to pay attention, then design can be, for me, the wrong kind of control, the too-tight grip, the difference between authoritarian and auteur.

When I took my faculty teaching job in North Carolina, I had just been at another institution that felt out of my control – a very small college in the plains of North-Central Iowa where I'd made a decent splash in a tiny pond, just in time for the 2008 financial crisis to hit and the college's major donor to pull support. It is here I learned that the prospect of losing my job was a kind of mortal annihilation I was unprepared to process in any healthy way. Strung out on back-to-back-to-back theatre projects, and a dad to a two-year old (and another baby on the way), I moved from barely sleeping to not sleeping, from frustrated to angry. I'd learn years later that this anger was sadness – mourning, really. As the financial crisis unfolded, the college sold itself to a for-profit company with a very different way of working. I registered them as corporate bullies, the very emblem of the establishment I became an artist to challenge. Some of them were corporate bullies, but I know now I was primed to see them all that way. I was in a constant state of panic for well over a year before I received an offer from the university where I now work.

Taking the job in North Carolina was a relief and an escape
and what I thought was a kind of grace extended by the Universe
or by God or by the impossible work of submitting something like
seventy applications. My family had vacationed in North Carolina
when I was growing up, stopping in the Smokies on our way to
family friends in the center of the state. These friends often took us
to a beach house on the coast – North Myrtle or Oak Island. I was
young, but I remember adventures of all sorts, from miniature golf
to very strange barbecue – all NC barbecue is strange to a normal
person from Kansas City – to getting caught in a squall on a long,
long walk down the beach. Turns out almost all those trips took us
right through where I now live. I often describe living in North Carolina like going to summer camp. I experience a lot of it – especially
when I can be outdoors – as vacation. It is a wonder of a greenhouse,
this place. Taking the job was a kind of grace, I thought.

My experience, though, was not graceful. Instead, I encountered
bullies – real ones, the kind that say the worst things they think
about you and the worst things you think about yourself both
behind your back and to your face. I witnessed interpersonal wars
between faculty members where students were weaponized. I got
dragged into those wars. My job – again, an emblem of my worth
and existence – was threatened repeatedly. Those kinds of threats
were made good on with other faculty members. There were screaming matches at program meetings. Long, nasty emails. Insults. Slurs.
You name it. The closest I've been able to describe that period in my
life was what happens when you see cartoon villains do their thing.

I should have left, but I didn't. Others did, pretty regularly those
first couple of years. Instead, I wrote copious notes and fired off
emails to administrators and hung on for dear life.

This was trauma, plain and simple. My background made my
experience of it much, much worse, but it would have been very bad

no matter what. For years, I couldn't drive up to my parking spot at my office without being overcome by a physiological reaction – anxiety on steroids. I sat in my office waiting for that day's drama to unfold.

This is around the time I started to get really good at design. I moved offices down the hall and put in some weird stuff – drapey fabrics in the windows, weird objects I've collected, some Buddhist prayer flags, some home-made art. This helped – it was me asserting control in a situation over which I had no control – but it did not turn the bullies into saints. The patterns were the problem.

It was not until one summer – not that long ago – when, burnt out and experiencing my kind of seasonal depression, I walked into my boss's office with a list of Big Asks. On this list, which I developed with a personal business coach, was that I needed to move offices – physically, geographically, and the hell out of the building I was in. The list included a lot of other things – ways of making space for me personally and experientially at work. And almost all of my list was granted right away, like it was supposed to have been that way all along.

It turns out that there was not actually another office for me. Instead, I got a practice room, less than half the size of my prior tiny office. The room had no windows – my earlier offices had floor-to-ceiling windows overlooking a courtyard. At 11am, the choir rehearsed across the hall – loudly. In the afternoons, the band rehearsed – very loudly. It was not ideal, but it was right. I drove a different way to work. I parked in a different spot. I decorated the office a bit with some colored lights. Less than two weeks after turning over my list – a design plan for my continued life at my job, really – a significant bully in our work ecosystem resigned.

See, that had been the unwritten thing on the list – the thing over which I had no control. As soon as I'd started to make space for my own personal bonfire experience, however, this person saw the party wasn't for them. I now sit in that person's office. It's bigger than my other two, on the ground floor where you're more likely to see people. I cleared out a bunch of that person's stuff – twenty years' worth – put up my colored lights, brought in a nice sofa and chair, and hung pictures of trees.

All this to say that it is possible to design your way out of a problem as long as you're not trying to control your way out of a problem.

The Work – the Deep Work – is designing the bonfire experience and consciously composing the Controlled Burn. I'm using design here in a few senses. Design can be:

- A plan ("the designs for my house")
- A decoration ("the design of my doorknob")
- An embodied practice ("my design work")

The first sense – design as a plan – conveys the idea of control and conscientiousness, while the second sense – design as decoration – could just as easily be the product of a flight of whimsy or spark of inspiration. Design, therefore, is both necessary and needless. In the third sense, design is The Work itself, moving from fires of danger to ones of delight.

Designing the bonfire experience is not really about designing the fire. Instead, it's about designing what's around the fire – in space and time and bodies – so that the Work works. My dad was an Eagle Scout in his younger days, and my wife is a lifetime Girl Scout with the vaunted Gold Award. These people stack their wood just so and I love them for it. I'm different. I want the wood arrangement to look generally like it will catch fire, and then I just want it to burn.

The fire itself is a beautiful thing for me, along with what happens around it.

The Work of the bonfire experience is about planning and possibility together – creating in space and time and bodies the chance for magic to happen.

Planning a Controlled Burn is planning for death and life at the same time. Please forgive my foray into the forests of cliche for a moment. Stuff has to burn so that a new, life-giving experience can emerge. At bonfires, we burn trees so that stories and warmth and light can emerge around these dead things. In controlled burns in forests, we burn little shrubs and plants and vines so that the sturdier, more established trees will not be threatened by wildfire. In my neck of the woods – the Sandhills of North Carolina – we have a lot of longleaf pines whose cones of seeds will only activate and take root when exposed to fire. Near my backyard fire pit, I have to have both deadwood and bare ground – scraping away leaves and pine straw in a radius around the pit itself so that only the right stuff will catch fire. To even have a fire pit, I have to be willing to give up some land that might otherwise grow perfectly fine grass. I have to be willing to let this little place scar, blackened like the ground and tree trunks of a controlled burn. When we are the things that are burning – or when we are doing the Work of Controlled Burning and bonfires – we, too, have to prepare ourselves for the kinds of deaths that allow for new life.

The Work, for me, has a few essential components:

- *Physically remove yourself from the current place.* A bonfire cannot take place next to the tinder of our homes, work, and daily activities without setting them on fire or becoming part of their patterns. A bonfire experience works because it is different from those things.

- *Shape the new space in a meaningful way.* Thin out the space – clear it of garbage. Bring decorations. Bring menu items. Bring people together. Form a community, even if it is for an evening.
- *Immerse yourself in the new experience.* Engage all the senses – breathe the smoke, eat the wood-fired food, take in the light.
- *Sit.* I mean this literally. Sit down. By sitting, I don't just mean you're comfortable and dissociated into your chair, but that you're ready to receive what's coming – warmth, stories, belonging.
- *Burn.* Consume, consciously and conscientiously, the dead stuff – the fake, the artificial, the pretend, the performative. Ask the burning questions. Chase the spark of inspiration. Allow yourself to light and be lit. Burning is a design feature of the bonfire, not a flaw. Burning is hot, messy, and can only be controlled to a certain extent, no matter the intention.
- *Tell stories.*

What I hope you're hearing is that we're not after a mindset change – at least not *only* a mindset change. That is like asking, very politely, for the fire to stop burning. Instead, we are after a change in *experience* – a change in our bodies. Design is a mindset change in action and a way to make manifestation matter – literally. It is the list of things you need to enact in the world *and* the doing of them *and* the digressions and adventures along the way. Design works both as we enact the present, minding the Controlled Burns of the moment, and as we engage The Work of designing the future so that even the wildest of fires will come under control over time.

I hasten to add that sometimes – maybe even most of the time – it is exceedingly difficult to do any of the things I mention above, such as physically moving from one place to another. The distance from my back door to my fire pit is about sixty feet, and that is good enough. Some of you may not have that privilege. In these cases, you do the absolute best you can to travel, shape the space, and immerse yourself in it, even if that "travel" is just imaginary, and shaping the space is just a shuffle of furniture. The point is to change what your body experiences and the paths it takes to get there.

I also want to say that design – even as an embodied practice – does not have to be something where you are the designer. It can also be experiencing someone else's design. And if they are good at it, their work will transport you, immerse you, cause you to sit in awe, burn in wonder, and listen carefully for the stories at play.

Whether designed or discovered, when you do The Work, you are requiring your body to confront new habits, new perspectives, and new ways of experiencing the world. The rest is just waiting for the magic to happen.

Disobedience & Disorientation

Controlled Burning is a kind of intentional disobedience. Such disobedience creates an experience that is necessarily different from all the other kinds of experiences we have for whatever stretches of time precede this one. When we design our own bonfire experiences, we are doing something that anticipates our bodies doing something they aren't used to doing – bonfires are exceptions in life, defiant moments of possibility and magic. When we stumble upon bonfires in our lives, they themselves are disobedient – potentially dangerous, always risky features on a landscape that is otherwise not on fire. Even the controlled burns of forestry are meant only for odd times in certain seasons – disobediently and defiantly burning what it is sensible not to burn.

"Disobedience is the beginning of Self."[4] Carl Jung called this process "differentiation," part of the Deep Work of becoming an individual rather than a member of the nameless masses.[5] Just as the bonfire is light standing against the darkness, heat against the cold, calm against a world of business, and community against a landscape of solitude, Controlled Burning by individuals and communities and in the experiences they create represents defiance.

As an artist and professional contrarian, this disobedience is easy for me to understand: I am broke when others are not, for instance. All kidding aside, in art and in the art of argument – public discourse – I *feel* on a daily basis what it is like to disobey. When the world is consuming, I am creating. When the world is thickening with garbage and noise, it is my role to thin it out and cut it back. When the world is full of unbridled celebration, it is my task to point out the advantage-taking and coldness of heart at the fringes of the party. When the world is suffering, it is my job to point out the grace at work. When the audience is enjoying the warmth and glow of a performance, it's my duty to be contemplating strike. Bonfire people work in a world of opposites.

The result of the Work is conscious disorientation. We can design the opposites or discover them – new pathways for our bodies to move, unfamiliar sensory experiences – "adventures" as I call them. This disorientation is necessary for the magic to happen. When our bodies experience things differently, our thoughts and feelings change. Our own perspective shifts. Our impulses give way to openness. In this way, disorientation is good – like our pupils dilating back to the dark world after time in the light of the fire, like our stories and relationships working in new ways on ourselves and each other.

We owe it to each other to be different – to disobey the hypnotic lull of our daily lives and the panic of our out-of-control fires – and to engage the world as great disorienters, shifting the landscape and making moments of transformation. Death into life. Mindlessness into care. Solitude into community. Secrets into stories.

Part 2

Firestarters

Thinning Spaces, Kindling Connections

Making the Metaphorical Bonfire

The rest of this book is very different – at least in form – from what's come before. What follows is a set of stories, embodied design practices, and other acts of death, delight, design, and disobedience, with some specific regard for how trauma was processed in my own mind, body, and story. Whereas the first part of the book has been a reflection and a bit of a how-to on Controlled Burning, what's coming is part of The Work itself, the making of the metaphorical bonfire. These "firestarters" are and aren't connected. You could, as I did, make a different bonfire with each one. I'll say something I've said before in a different way: my ways ought not be your ways. It is here that the "how to" stops and the testament begins. These firestarters are things that worked for me: the Deep Work, and the stories I've not shared before in quite this way. The point is not that my journey is yours, but that something in my journey might kindle a flame for you.

Importantly, what follows is weird – sometimes veering into "woo," those esoteric things that normal people squint at sideways.

I am not, by nature, a woo person. I drink beer, watch American football, follow politics, and play video games. What's more, I've not become particularly more woo in the time after I've done the things I'll describe. There's no question, however, that this stuff is weird. It may not be your thing, and that is just fine. What matters for me is that it is *different*, *disobedient*, and *disorienting*. Some of it is *delightful*. Whenever you are lighting your own bonfires, it is important that your Work is those things, too. In this regard, you will be weird in your own way.

The word I often use to describe all this different, disobedient, disorienting, death-defying, delightful stuff that feels a little weird at times is *magic*. Magic is what happens when the party is right, when the bonfire experience is happening, and when the Controlled Burn is burning. You'll see what I mean.

Thinning Spaces

"Most religions, certainly mine, teach that God is available every-where. Why, then, should I go to Iona to find God rather than my bedroom closet?" – Daniel Taylor, *In Search of Sacred Places*

Where does or can magic happen? Are thin places where magic happens? What the hell is a thin place? Something of a sacred place, a *thin* place is one where spiritual magic happens – the site of the bonfire, the ground of the Controlled Burn. While the notion of a thin place emerges from Celtic Christianity, my work here is to introduce it as a concept that can apply to a variety of temporal, local places that reveal a deeper, more mysterious, cosmic reality and to share my experiences encountering thin places.

For example, after walking through a grave-strewn churchyard in London near the Smithfield meat market a few blocks north of Saint Paul's Cathedral, one enters an unimposing set of doors, certainly ecclesiastical in nature, but unremarkable given the architectural smorgasbord of central London. The church exterior has been stitched together with brick application from the 20th century and the earlier Victorian era, with glimpses of earlier periods peeking out here and there. Unless one is a Christian, a London historian, or an especially inquisitive adventurer, there's no particular reason to stroll into this church. There are hundreds of historical churches nearby, most with much more impressive external identities, not the least of which is Saint Paul's and the many, many churches rebuilt by the distinguished architect Christopher Wren in the decades after the Great Fire of London in 1666. But as one sneaks through the doors, turns left a few paces, and then follows the building as it opens up to a magnificent sanctuary, there is an unmistakable sense of awe that overtakes the observer. Incense hangs in the air between windows. Light spills between Norman arches built in the middle of the twelfth century. Saint Bartholomew the Great Church is something of an anomaly in London. Spared from the Great Fire by virtue of existing outside the city walls, away from where most of the apocalyptic damage occurred, surviving the World War II bombs that flattened many of the other buildings of comparable stature, yet suffering from years of disrepair, only a few buildings of its age survive. Founded by Rahere, a somewhat legendary figure in English history who emerges as a priest, monk, courtier, and court jester, the church is haunting, magical, and thin. There is something going on there that is more than the sum of its historical and architectural parts – at least there was for me when I first encountered the incredible, stirring vista as I turned the corner into the sanctuary.

The nave of Saint Bartholomew the Great Church,
London.
Greg Fiebig

For me, Saint Bart's is a thin place. This term, thin place, is one I first encountered on the lips of an Episcopal priest a handful of years ago as she described what I've come to learn as an element of Christian contemplative practice, a meditative life of both quiet engagement with the inner world of oneself and yearning openness to the mystic possibilities of creation. This priest likely encountered the concept in one of two ways. First, the notion of thin place emerged in Evangelical Christian thinking over the last small few decades, mostly through the Christian publishing, conference, and travel industries. Mainline and Evangelical churches have several touchpoints, including these industries, and the influence from one (usually the Evangelical church) seeps into the other. Second, the Episcopal church, America's Anglican spin-off, draws a rich spiritual ancestry back to the British Isles, often incorporating elements of Celtic Christian spirituality and practice into its identity and worship, not the least of which is its common use of the labyrinth, a Celtic invention evocative of the Eastern mandala that facilitates contemplative prayer walks.

So what is a thin place? My notion of a thin place emerges from would-be-sacred soup, a mix of the mystical and imagined past, contemporary practice, and a yearning practitioner. Mary DeMuth, an Evangelical Christian writer, evokes this imagined past as a contemporary practice, noting that Celts defined a thin place as "a place where heaven and the physical world collide, one of those serendipitous territories where eternity and the mundane meet".[6] Thin "describes the membrane between the two worlds, like a piece of vellum, where we see a holy glimpse of the eternal," where "ancients whisper their wisdom near the ruins of a church or the craggy outcropping of a rock ... a doorway to the fairy-tale netherworld." DeMuth's Christian language is an encoded version of Jeffrey Kripal's notion of the magical "night world," a side of reality that materialist and empirical knowledge cannot (fully) access.[7] Kripal's scholarly work focuses on mystical literature and the history of Western esotericism from gnosticism to New Age religions. In other words, a thin place might be thought of as one with shamanic identity, proclivity, or access to this other "thin" or "night" world. It is the place where the magic happens, or at least where it can happen.

Uncomfortably, perhaps, Kripal's Romantic Vision of an unconscious or subconscious Truth, a "nonrational or superrational" metanarrative, fits squarely within the mystical and modern Christian worlds, both Evangelical and Mainline, Celtic past and naïve present.[8] Christianity sees the world, at least in part, Platonically, as a division between what we can experience in sense and place and time—the empirically observable material world, and the world of the spirit, a "nonlocal and nontemporal" reality of an emerging cosmic consciousness.[9] The Evangelical and many Mainline churches would perhaps describe this as an unfolding of God's will across the story of humanity, while more contemplative traditions have long adopted a more panentheistic view of the cosmic story, most notably in the work of Fr. Richard Rohr and his Center for Action and Contemplation, but also in authors such as Deepak Chopra.[10] For Christians in tune with any number of spiritual theologies, Kripal speaks their truth and reifies it from an ironically humanist perspective. Christian blogger Gabby Llewelyn, alongside DeMuth, sees the thin place as an exact spot where the material world and the magic world commingle, describing a spot, "where the gap between our reality and God's stops feeling wide and uncrossable. Thin enough to hear a whisper, to see through to the other side".[11] Ernesto De Martino suggests that the shaman is a sort of *magical Christ*, a redemptive bridge for the community between the material and spirit worlds; in this way, the thin place is also like that bridge or a locus for a shamanic, Christian, magical transformation for those present.[12] At least those who talk about thin places present the encounter in terms of the mystical and the heavenly.

In this sense, thin places are where mutants are made. Kripal, Eric Wargo, Alejandro Jodorowsky, and Rachael LeValley[13] contemplate mutants in humanity, cosmology, science (Kripal and Wargo), science fiction (Wargo), Buddhism (Kripal, Wargo, and Jodorowsky), and experimental practice (Wargo's Scientology and Jodorowsky's and LeValley's Psychomagic) — all but Jodorowsky neglecting that this has been Christianity's view of itself from the beginning.[14] In the Evangelical and some Mainline views, mutants are the converted, evolved from a life of sin into new, immortal life. In other Mainline and contemplative views, mutants are the beings that are part of and awaken to the cosmic unfolding of creation, the goal being something like Jodorowsky's realizing of the cosmic reality. Of course, most Christians don't call themselves mutants as a matter of course—the term mutant often carries negative and non-religious associations—but many do engage the necessary transformation as a matter of practice, whether it be in the metaphysical (and physical?) conversion of bread and wine into Christ's body and blood or in the upfitting of the personal soul or in communal activism. Mutation is the name of the game and sacred space the gameboard. Sanctuaries like Saint Bart's, the British-Celtic island and ancient monastery of Iona, Biblical locations, and even the interior world of the mutants themselves may be thought of, and of course many are designed, as sacred spaces. But not every space is thin. Not every space does the magical "trick" of mutation for the observer. Is Christ especially on the island of Iona, or on the craggy outcropping of Skellig Michael? Is it especially in the Blue Mosque? Is that even the question? A Christ who is especially anywhere presents a problem for the shamanic and Christian panentheism and for Kripal's cosmic connectedness.

A materialist, empiricist view of the thin space would account for this. De Martino calls attention to the possibility of shamanic suggestion.[15] Knowing the place is known for the thin, liminal, transformational experience, as a pilgrim to Iona would, is both a possible explanation for the many testimonials that emerge about it and good tourism strategy for a remote island off the west coast of Scotland. Winifred Gallagher, observing Michael Persinger, suggests physical, if subtle, environmental phenomena that stimulate the observer in unique ways, from electromagnetic fields to seismic activity.[16] Persinger also points to electrochemical and nervous system responses in the human body that incline it toward an experience of a place as sacred, with the range of responses accounting for whether or not a given person could experience something sacred at a certain locale. Most compellingly, Persinger suggests in Gallagher that much of the work of sacred space, such as altars, comes from their abrupt difference from the rest of static reality. A thin space is thin because other spaces are thick. Or we are. Perhaps we experience the "emotional residue" of a place, a kind of scientific phenomena where we can detect the "energies" left by prior occupants, sometimes chemically. Perhaps thin places are just quiet, natural, and de-electrified, meeting Persinger's criteria of an abrupt difference from the modern, Western experience. Perhaps this is simple nostalgia or object bonding. I have Scots-Irish heritage; my grandmother told me, and so here I am in the homeland. I'm a Christian, and this is an old, Christian place. My house is wood and steel; this is rock. I'm from brutally hot North Carolina, and the chilly fog here is, in Kripal's possible terms, otherworldly. It isn't my world, where my observational senses have thickened to protect me from the onslaught of phone calls and electronic messages and brightly lit rooms and artificial surfaces, but a world that invites me into its remarkable difference. Or perhaps "the experience of a thin place feels special because words fail," and I cannot situate the experience in any available frame of reference.[17]

A magical view might require the spiritual or magical openness of the viewer, an access point to the spirit world, or a shortcut to awakening. Thin places present themselves, in part, as both within and distinct from a wider definition of sacred space. Norbert Brockman suggests that sacred spaces are where "the seeker encounters the holy and, through rituals, meditation, and revelation, experiences a call to move beyond the self".[18] David Douglas admits these places might not emerge in an established religious or spiritual tradition, but "could simply be places that we personally hold dear—places that bear an importance for us...that feed us on some deeper level than simply the ordinary".[19] Both Brockman and Douglas point to spaces from cathedrals and monasteries to indigenous burial grounds, ancient sites of revelation, or stone circles from the prehistoric past. These places are soaked in intent, meditative energy, and generations of spirits haunting and thinning the veil between the physical world and the other one while scores of pilgrims walk ever deeper into the holy experience within. The thin place is a supernatural one because that is what it has proven itself to be.

If there is a difference between what can be accounted for empirically and what I experience as a human being undergoing magical transformation, it may not matter or we may not care. To me, the magic works. Whether standing in Saint Bart's or Iona or a sweat lodge or on the floor of a quiet room with others undertaking a journey to discover a spirit helper, or whether I've gone, as a therapist might invite me, to a "calm, safe place," the magical or sensory effect is the same, perhaps. "Explanations aren't merely useless; they threaten to get in the way," notes Oliver Burkeman, who experienced a thin space in a dark room in Milan while gazing upon DaVinci's *Last Supper*. He notes there might not be much use in a psychology questionnaire of people who've just visited the Grand Canyon. Wonder and strangeness might not come in such packages or even on the thinnest of spaces, if such spaces are pages of questionnaires or essays like this one.

The thin space, both with and without its material and physical explanations, upsets and challenges our expectations. Eric Weiner, a travel writer, notes that thin spaces cause us to "lose our bearings, and find new ones," as "we are jolted out of old ways of seeing the world, and therein lies the transformative magic of travel".[20] Weiner stumbles upon a common thread in thinking about thin spaces: one has to get there, as with the mental journey of a Buddhist or a shamanic journey inward to the spirits worlds or the Hero's Journey of Jung and Campbell or this foot in front of that one on a labyrinth or a hike to an *other* place. Travel has the potential for ushering in the liminality required to encounter a thin place, moving us to the strange threshold where we are in neither the material nor the magical reality.

Saint Bart's revels in its strangeness. Saint Bart's is old enough, as are many parishes in England, that it is both historically Anglican and Catholic, built centuries before Luther, Calvin, and the Wesley brothers reshaped the English-speaking Church. This is part of what sets it apart from its nearby cousins. Even a sister church nearby, Saint Bartholomew the Less, does not seem to carry the same spiritual weight as Old Saint Bart. Saint Paul's and most of the other nearby parishes, many of them Wren inventions, are decidedly Baroque structures featuring wide vistas, clear windows, and white paint. Wren, a product of the then-Reformed Anglican tradition, saw his London rebuilding project as an opportunity to make a theological statement. Abandoning the medieval and more mystical tradition of the burned-out churches lost in the Great Fire, each with stained glass, rich painting, and color, Wren restated Christian theology in architectural terms. The clear windows confront the worshiper with the natural, sinful world in need of saving. The abandonment of these glass icons and the white walls do not infect, in Reformed thinking, the mind of the worshiper. Wren's work was, in many ways, the final realization of a project that had begun over a century earlier with the reforms of the Church under Henry VIII and Edward V, each of whom, in different ways and for different reasons, called for the stripping of Catholic iconography and ornamentation in parishes throughout the realm. They couldn't pull down the medieval stained glass, not until the Great Fire. And though Saint Bart's now has clear windows, the result of many years of disrepair and the occasional calamity, these sit within decidedly medieval windows, a callback to the earlier age. Saint Bart's characteristic Norman arches also call back to an even earlier identity of the Norman invaders—a French-speaking conglomeration with a Viking heritage. Norman architecture is a signal of an older national identity, older than the Gothic architecture that arrived in subsequent centuries, and certainly older than the neo-Roman styles brought by the Baroque period. It's also a less capable architecture than Wren's or the Gothic architect, unable to support the wide or vaulted ceilings of each. Old Saint Bart's is narrow, strange, different, older, and these features work together to set it apart for the observer, to make it thin. Built in part as a hospital, and now with a graveyard out front, I wonder if St. Bart's is an especially spirited place. Its doorways and pathways trod by generations of anointed clergy and open-hearted, seeking worshippers seeking communion, I wonder if the space itself has undergone a kind of transubstantiation, a swap of the mundane elements of rock and glass and smoke for saintly versions of those things. Founded by a royal fool, the trickster figure at the center of courtly life, I wonder if St. Bart's is soaked in historical mischief, a manifestation of the temporal sleight of hand or linguistic trick set into motion by Rahere so long ago.

* * *

Thinness can also be experienced at Carver's Creek State Park. Carver's is relatively new to the North Carolina park system, cut out a few years ago from the lands belonging to Fort Bragg, the world's purported largest military installation and home to the United States' Army's 82nd Airborne Division and a Special Operations Command. It has two access points, including one off Long Farm Valley Road, directly across from Bragg's Clay Target Center, which emits the sound of percussive gunfire, both single shot and the rapid-fire rattle of something one imagines to be a machine gun. Wander too far off the path and you'll find yourself in one of Bragg's many subdivisions of on-base housing. Carver's Creek is also part-way in the flight path of Pope Army Airfield, and as one wanders past one of the park's main features, the slowly decaying winter home of James Rockefeller, a relation of John D. Rockefeller, you'll see the reconstruction of a small dam that was washed out by Hurricane Florence. Bulldozers and generators hum, even on a Saturday, in hopes of the pond's resurrection as a modest fishing spot and hopeful draw for the park's tiny staff. Between the planes and the sound of bullets and the huge machinery, it's hard to get around the idea that we are at the heart of the Empire in all its capitalistic and militaristic glory.

Ninety minutes away, up Highways 87 and 42 and west on 64 past Asheville, lies Thomasville Buddhist Center, a building that, like its chief operator, has undergone a remarkable transformation in recent years. Once known as Saint Stephen's Missionary Baptist Church, Thomasville Buddhist Center (TBC) is a brightly painted brick and cinder block construction with a modest garden out front, several prayer flags and garlands strewn about the yard, and several representations of the Buddha in statue and printed form. Inside, TBC's lobby is dark. To the right is a restroom and to the left a small kitchen with a table and chairs. Walk ahead and you're in the main room of the center, perhaps what was once either a sanctuary or fellowship hall. Now, the room is a multi-use space. While a couple of sofas rest in the near left corner and a computer and desk in the near right corner, much of the rest of the room is open, save a partition about two-thirds of the way into the space, partly masking a dais on which rests a massage table and some implements for one of the room's many uses as a martial arts studio. On the near side of the partition, the room changes identities partly based on the day. For weekly Intro to Buddhism classes and other educational initiatives, the space contains conventional folding tables. On other days, the tables are cleared to make way for padded flooring for martial arts classes and practice. For Sunday mornings, cushions and supports are added for those who attend dharma talks at the Center's communal gathering. One constant is a station with a knee-level podium and several implements of Buddhist practice, from bells to prayer wheels. Behind the station is an image of Buddha, several photographs, a mandala tapestry, and other effects. Here and all over the partition, just as outside, there are bright colors on fabric and cardboard, artificial flowers and objects firmly establishing the space as a Buddhist one. On most days when the Center is open, incense wafts in from its perch near an open window, taking prime advantage of the cross breeze. TBC is an eruption of sensory experiences, both visual, auditory, and aromatic. Add to that the customary sangha (community) vegan meal on Sundays and a recent decision by the TBC board to live off the grid (and without air conditioning), and one, upon lingering in TBC even for moments, encounters a strange, transportive world.

Emerging from both worlds, the empire and the liminal and marginal space of TBC, is Heiwa No Bushi (formerly Bushi Yamato Damashii), the Center's abbot. Bushi, as most call him, is the former pastor of the former progressive Baptist congregation held on the site, a retired Marine with at least one tour in Iraq to his credit. Then known as T. (Torrence) Marquis Ramsey, Bushi grew up in the Baptist church, following his grandmother, a relatively anomalous woman preacher from Florida, to the ministry. Ramsey obtained some academic titles – either real or paper, it's difficult to tell – while pursuing the ministry and exploring Buddhist practice. In 2008, he publicly gave up the ministry to pursue Buddhism's Middle Way. He freely shares that some of the transition from Christian to Buddhist was the result of him processing the unexpected death of his child, a daughter. After years as a retreatant, something of a full-time Buddhist student, explorer, and practitioner, Bushi emerged in recent years with the BodhiChristo ("Awakened Christ") movement, a new Buddhist lineage that is both fully Buddhist and fully Christian. Lineages, in the Buddhist tradition, are something like a distinct set of practices and beliefs based on teacher-student relationships, common life, and the empowerment, transmission, and extension of core concepts over time.

BodhiChristo has been on full display in some narrow progressive Christian and Buddhist circles for several years, perhaps most notably at the Wild Goose Festival, an annual conference that includes those like Bushi alongside Christian contemplatives, shamans, pagans (yes, Christian pagans), and more mainline, if progressive, ministers and public figures. Among the most notable of these figures is a group called The Liturgists. The Liturgists started initially as a podcast between Michael Gungor, a charismatic, Evangelical Christian worship leader and Christian music frontman who has since abandoned much of his Christian beliefs in favor of a more Buddhist model, and Mike McHargue, also known as "Science Mike," a mainline Christian who was de-ordained as a deacon in the Southern Baptist Church several years ago after declaring himself an atheist and who has since returned to the church after a mystical experience of hearing the voice of God while walking on the beach in California. Since the founding of the podcast, The Liturgists organization grew to include other co-hosts, regular gatherings, on-line courses, and a variety of media offerings. The Liturgists today is no longer at its peak influence because of a rather public schism between Gungor and McHargue, but it still boasts a sizable pod-cast and weekly gatherings. The Liturgists serves a community of inquiring atheists and agnostics as well as Christians, often Evangel-ical or conservative, through spiritual deconstruction to the tune of millions of podcast downloads and an ample international following that leans heavily on being affirming of LGBTQI+ persons, mind-fulness, meditation, and the validation of spiritual engagement as parts of its core identity. In February of 2019, in an episode of the podcast on Buddhism, The Liturgists co-hosts interviewed Bushi on his approach to Buddhism and elements of his own spiritual decon-struction. The interview put an instant, and international, spotlight on Bushi and the TBC, making him something of an overnight celebrity, at least within The Liturgists' sphere of influence.

The interview is also where I first heard of Bushi in February of 2019, and where I need to share at least part of my story here as the decidedly biased observer and witting participant in the exploration into the concept of "thin space" that is nominally the reason I'm writing. In February of 2019, I was in the throes of mental health recovery. I had just finished a production of the musical *Sweeney Todd* for a theatre company and operate where I played the title character, a mass-murdering barber. During the production, I suf-fered significant psychological and emotional challenges stemming from the weight of the show, the nature of the role, intense inter-personal drama between me and some other members of the theatre company that had run on for months, and psychological diagnoses of mental disorders running back several months, anxiety disorder running back a few years, and later major depressive disorder, ADHD, and another trauma-related disorder. That January, I was on my third adjustment of a drug meant to address some symptoms while adding a stimulant to begin to address ADHD. Cognitive Be-havior Therapy, which I'd been undertaking for several months, was having minimal effect. I'd fought with my Episcopal church leader-ship as part of the crisis and was rarely attending weekly worship. I'd resigned my ceremonial job in the church as a verger, which is a kind of worship leader and coordinator. January and early February was some shit, I have to tell you, and the events and chemical cocktails resulted in episodes where I would suddenly burst into tears, or rage at people I usually liked, or break off into patterns of fiery behavior. I identified then, even in the stupor of my body's ongoing trauma response, that I was in crisis. Without the benefit of my entire biog-raphy, I hope this is enough to give you the context in which I, the son of a former Southern Baptist preacher and someone who tuned into The Liturgists with great intrigue, greeted the arrival of Bushi in my ears during a car ride. I liked what I heard, even so much that I found myself shouting in delightful agreement. Bushi's background and mine aligned, to some degree, and that wasn't the least of it.

I first visited TBC late the next month and again several times over the next few months, connected with Bushi's sangha (practicing community) online, and was given transmission and empowerment as a student in the BodhiChristo lineage. These latter activities, the transmission and empowerment, took place in a ceremony between some flag-adorned trees on the wide grounds of a cabin site in Hot Springs, North Carolina, during one morning of the 2019 Wild

Goose Festival, where I traveled to from Indiana, about 8 hours one way, where I'd taken a gig directing a play. The cabin site abuts the French Broad River. As a student of Bushi and member of the BodhiChristo sangha, the main focus for me and the other students is to engage in daily meditation practice of an ideal 30 minutes in the morning and 30 minutes in the evening with slowly included Tibetan or Zen Buddhist physical salutations, a dedicated physical practice (most choose a martial art, yoga, or reiki), and intense study of one's own mind. The sangha attracts members from across the southeast as well as other parts of the country and includes members of The Liturgists creative and support staff.

On one level, Buddhist practice as articulated in BodhiChristo and TBC strike me as merely different from Christian practice, and the difference is objectively inconsequential. TBC's sangha is Christianity's parish or congregation. Meditation is prayer. Dharma talks are sermons. Sutras, among other writings, are scripture. Weekly community meals happen at TBC as they might at my local Episcopal church. There's a hierarchy. Buddhist icons, banners, prayer flags, social activities like yoga class, clergy, and so on each have a correlative in a Christian space. Buddhism has bells and incense and prayer wheels and mandalas; Christianity has bells and organs and incense and genuflections and labyrinths. My empiricist brain goes to work and decides the structures are the same: material representations of an attempt to access an Ultimate Reality. The emotional or spiritual opening I feel at TBC emerges from the fact that it, like St. Bart's is so different from the landscapes—literal, spiritual, and metaphorical—that surround it. TBC looks different, outside and in. Bushi, an African American, is my first such spiritual leader. The sangha is the most diverse spiritual community I've taken part in. The drive to Thomasville, two hours from my home in Fayetteville, is a blur of green longleaf pines and a smattering of rural small towns, from Sanford to Ramseur to Asheboro, altogether serving as the basis for a liminal experience like a plane ride to London or a long walk from my hotel to St. Bart's or a ferry ride to the far end of Iona. Bushi, in his dharma robes, looks like a priest of a sort, upending and unsettling in a way. But I'm a theatre director and the son of a former Southern Baptist pastor: I get costumes and performance. There's a man underneath those robes and a stage, of sorts, underneath that station in the main room. TBC, in the empirical and analytical parts of my brain, is just new wine in an old wineskin.

And yet, TBC and intentional Buddhist space, like the site between the trees where I received transmission and empowerment, is also a thin, magical space. I say this subjectively, of course. I can see Bushi in Hot Springs for the length of a hello or a long conversation and it is not the same. I can meditate, successfully one might say, in my home or on a quiet beach or during a long walk down a trail of the Blue Ridge mountains, but it is not the same. Of course this may just be me: I'm anticipating too much, clinging too hard to the expectation that I should feel *here*, wherever here is, closing any spiritual opening I might encounter rather than fully experiencing the Buddhist notion of *this*. Maybe I'm doing it wrong when I'm not at TBC or with Bushi at the ceremony. Maybe I'm too new to *this*. Maybe I'm undisciplined in meditation practice. Or maybe it's the magic of Bushi's spaces and intention. Perhaps he is what I think he is: a healer, a shaman, one with the metaphorical magic juice that's been sprinkled often and intentionally at TBC and other spaces he designs.

In the strictest sense, Buddhist philosophy would not allow for this. As one member of the sangha put it to me in an interview, "My practice is giving and creating space no matter where I am and what I'm dealing with. This allows my dharma practice to be carried internally wherever I go".[21] Buddhist meditation, particularly at the beginning stages, focuses on dependent causation, nothing-ness, not-self, *this*ness, and death. Dependent causation is the idea that *nothing*, not even the self, exists. A common example used for contemplation and meditation is the idea of a flower. The flower can be broken down, first of all. Its petals can be taken off, its stem cut, it can shrivel and die. When, exactly, does it lose its identity, or suchness ("this is such flower") as a flower? More powerfully, the flower does not exist at all on its own. It does not exist without the sun, without photosynthetic processes, or without a seed, water, pollinators, pigments, stamen, pistils, and nutrients. Now, take any of those component parts. They, too, do not exist on their own. They are made of chemical reactions or molecules or elements or physical processes that are themselves dependent on other things going back in time and space to the untraceable beyond. So, too, with the human. For the Buddhist, there is no flower, no self, noth-ing except *this*, an awareness of the current moment and its present conditions, a kind of cosmic lens of perception that replaces the ego. Moreover, Buddhist meditative practice, and part of what Bushi requires of the sangha and of me, is an internal journey, an examina-tion of the mind, internal motivations, stress, anxiety, trauma, and their ultimate causes and conditions. The therapeutic implications are evident: if the flower does not exist, the anxiety does not exist. Mental strength and acuity, achieved through disciplined meditative practice, moves the practitioner to a state of suchness and presence. Because meditation is an inward journey, and because the physical world has a quality of nothingness about it, Buddhist philosophy would seem to suggest, as the sangha member above does, that place does not matter. Wherever I am is a perception that does not reflect the Ultimate Reality. There is no material. There is no place, there-fore there are no thin places. Hell, there is no me to experience no place. There is just *this*, a cosmic reality. The flip of that, of course, is that everything is a thin place, and my Self, uncompartmentalized and disintegrated into the cosmos, is *this*, the cosmos itself.

BodhiChristo, and Buddhism more broadly, are hardly so impractical. As in Christianity, there are representations and reminders of the cosmic reality. Buddha statues remind us of the Buddha himself, and whose path is one supposed to be followed. Icons of Buddhist deities, most grounded in Indian, Tibetan, and Chinese predecessors, invite us toward a quality of ideal understanding. Prayer bowls and bells invite us into mental clarity and re-centering. Everywhere there are visual and auditory reminders, the costumes and props and sound effects of Buddhist practice, meant to ease and facilitate and draw in the practitioner so that they are capable of the transformation and cosmic communion they seek. These tools, sacred as a eucharistic chalice or a stained glass window, sit in tension with Buddhist nothingness and the potentiality of awakening: the material and physical cues alert us to the inner and cosmic journeys. Space is one of these tools, as it is at TBC and many Buddhist temples, visual and auditory feasts in the material world that, as with churches and mosques and monasteries and synagogues and shamanic ritual sites, call us toward another realization or healing. Another member of the BodhiChristo sangha, speaking in an interview, describes such sites this way:

> I have cultivated my own house and grounds to be a place of practice. When they do not seem to be enough to settle me, I have some special spaces, places where I can reliably expect to enhance my sense of emotional stability and experience myself quieting down in order to better experience divine presence. The Baha'i Temple (the beauty of the structure and the gardens), Chinatown and Little India (eating good food and engaging people from other cultures), the ISKCON Temple (opportunity to chant and dance

corporately), a few churches (depending on the lighting and space considerations). All these spaces allow me to open my mind further to appreciate the beauty that is constantly trying to reveal itself in a fraught world.[22]

Bushi himself engages in this kind of intentional cultivation of sacredness in his spaces:

> In our everyday lives there are elements of the sacred. Fire, water, smoke, stone, air, nature, the unexplained. I bring all elements of the universe, in some form or another, into tangible placement around my heart (retreat space, home, etc.) as a reminder of my interbeing with these sacredly acknowledged elements.[23]

Bushi here is pointing to the cosmic reality he's attempting to access or awaken to. In one sense, he arranges the material world simply as the reminder. In another sense, he's engaging the material world to learn from it. He says, "I bring these elements into healing and mental spaces so that I might deeply immerse my energy into their wisdom and knowledge".[24] Bushi sees himself as a healer, or at least a facilitator of healing. Work with him, he admits, is therapeutic. After receiving my transmission and empowerment, he says the empowerment is to begin serious practice in the study of myself. His first question is whether I'm still in therapy. The impression I get is that I'm supposed to start there, looking deeply inward to get to the bottom of my shit. Bushi also encourages his students, followers, and inquirers to work on their spaces with the kind of intent he displays, saying he will often "encourage this same inclusivity [of material elements] into my corporate teachings and guidance, as these are essential to my own mental and energetic properties, in which I seek to educate my students and other adherents".[25]

The idea here is three-fold: one, that the thin space can be manufactured with intention; two, that the spiritual opening happens within the practitioner, and not outside it; three, and somewhat conversely, that the natural, material world contains within it potential magic or thinness or holy presence. In Buddhism and Christianity, this implies that the thin space is portable within the practitioner or so readily accessible in the natural world that it is just there. An associate of Bushi's, Mike Morrell, a self-described panentheist and contemplative, puts it this way:

> I feel ambivalent about the idea of 'thin places,' to be perfectly honest. It reminds me of certain streams of Christianity I grew up in, where people are begging God to show up. Isn't God already here? Panentheism, or even simple Omnipresence, would seem to indicate that God is everywhere - as the Christian tradition says, 'all in all,' 'in Whom we live, move, and have our being." I imagine Buddhism says similar things about the Buddha nature being everywhere; suchness being the same as form, if we but have eyes to see. And *that* is probably the other side of the dialectic: Buddhism says we need to Wake Up! Christianity says we need to experience Metanoia, a changing of the mind and heart, to see the Kingdom already 'at hand'.[26]

Morell suggests too that this waking up or metanoia, a Greek term describing religious conversion, can be crafted, saying "I think it's possible! If so, it's all about intention, and attention—tuning—into 'What is'... A subtle-but-real shift ... bringing our real presence to those rites and spaces where we expect to witness Spirit's real presence." At the same time, Morell thinks

> Sometimes thin spaces simply seem to *be*—especially in nature. One can feel more palpable Presence, and not even know why. Not intending to, it simply *is*. Maybe because those of previous generations bathed that space in meditation or prayer...who knows?

Morell's definitions allow, then, for two kinds of thin experiences, much like the second member of the sangha mentioned above, who both designs her own sacred space at home and stumbles upon them in her journeys in Chicago, or like the thinness I experienced as a function of walking through the shallow, rocky flow of the French Broad river next to Bushi's cabin, and the flag-adorned site and rituals of transmission and empowerment a few dozen yards in from the shore. The cosmic awakening happens in both places, and within me, perhaps. This is Jodorowsky's mutant emerging both as a theatrical panic and as a shamanic, psychomagical healing. The ritual is what Bushi does with his words and hands on my forehead and scalp, but it is also my openness as I stand the day before in the river, looking for rocks, both expecting and not expecting something cosmic and Ultimately Real to happen. It is also the turn of the corner into St. Bart's, not expecting anything to happen. Thin places, maybe, are recognitions of a panentheistic reality. The cosmos is revealing itself if we will look, but sometimes, it also insists that it be seen.

Scorched Earths

Weeks later, I'm making my way to Carver's Creek to check it out and to see if there's thin space there or can be made there. I've driven by the park entrance dozens of times on my way from Fayetteville to points north, and it is a common marker on my way to and from TBC: either I've just started the journey or I'm almost home. I have with me a backpack with tea, some of my Buddhist implements like a Tibetan singing bowl, mala beads, a beaded bracelet given to me by Bushi at the transmission and empowerment ceremony, and a small statue of Jesus, seated in the meditating position much more common to statues of Buddha. I have tea and incense. I have a copy of Jodorowsky's and LeValley's *Psychomagic*, flagged to his meditation exercises and his discussion of space in his Accelerated Course in Creativity, some clove oil, a pocket journal, my watch, and a few stones. Most of the stones I collected on a couple walks in the French Broad the month before. One of them has a mandala pattern my mother painted at my request. It isn't from the French Broad.

The preparatory materials.

First stop: Starbucks. Dirty tea. Much dirtier than the simple black tea in my growler. This one is Earl Grey and several shots of espresso, along with some almond milk.

Starbucks Empire.

Natural Elements from the Starbucks empire. It's relatively early on a Saturday, and I need to wake up chemically before I wake up spiritually, I think. Starbucks is a kind of self-care for the novice contemplative, maybe.

Carver's Creek access at Long Valley Farm is a gravel parking lot with an adjacent park headquarters, a small building with a couple of displays, and a variety of park materials. A park ranger is there, pointing out the park's features. The gravel lot opens up to a long, sandy path. On one side is a mixed forest of deciduous trees and the longleaf pines so emblematic of this part of the state. On the other side, wide meadows, overgrown with wildflowers and grasses.

Longleaf Pines.

The field.

A burst of yellow.

Pilgrim?

A visit of white.

The road travelled.

Partway down the path, on the meadow side, is a rusty metal gate, probably from the park's past life as rural farmland. On the fence is orange cautionary plastic. I'm reminded that orange is a sacred color in Buddhism. One of my readings many months before, I forget which one, says that if you encounter orange or red fabric on your path, you're to pick it up and tie it to a tree. Orange and red are the colors of monks' robes.

Orange like monks.

Just beyond, dead trees stick themselves out from the green background, alerting me to the life cycle of plants, all life, and my life.

A dead tree, among other things.

But this is me also reaching, grasping for meaning in a place I'm not feeling, not yet anyway. The walk is certainly poetic and symbolic. It has Jodorowsky's and Morell's and Bushi's principles at play, of course. I'm here as a clinician, yet I can't escape clinging to the idea that something should happen—butterflies, orange and yellow, the holy colors, start to flitter in the brush as I walk past.

A butterfly.

Another butterfly.

Near an informational sign a little way down sits a rock, brightly painted and with the words "A Million Dreams" on it. On the back is a bit of paper with text inviting me to share a photo of the rock on a website and then to re-hide it, like an Easter egg hunt. Just above lies a sign about the life cycle of forests and the role of controlled burning in forest management.

Signs.

Beyond the sign the lush, green, bright summer world of the park dissolves abruptly. The ground is black with char. There is no underbrush here as there had been to this point on my walk. The bottoms of the largest and most resilient trees are blackened from a recent fire.

Scorched earth.

Char.

Gradation.

Where the fire hasn't completely disintegrated the underbrush and smaller trees, they are yellowed from the intense heat. My shadow falls with the shadows of trees on the ground, black on black. Returning to the sandy path, I'm struck by the contrast here

of death and life and transformation. Killing something here while
life continues there. Letting part of a forest die so something can live,
like a caterpillar sewing a cocoon. Maybe I'm entering a meditative
space, I think, a place where a cosmic lesson is unfolding.

Contrasts.

Up and around the bend, the sandy path unfurls into mowed
green acreage around several buildings, the chief of which is the
park's cultural landmark, the Long Valley Farmhouse, adjacent to a
boathouse on what might otherwise be a sizable pond. The ranger
has told me the pond's dam was wiped out by Hurricane Florence.
The state is just now working on dam repairs. The pond might be
reborn in a year, she says. Meanwhile, the idyllic estate is governed
by big machinery, plastic, metal, and concrete. Even on a Saturday,
some of the machinery, perhaps a generator or two, hum not far

out of sight. A father and his child, kept in a stroller, hurriedly rush past me. The dad is on a run and has the appearance of a soldier from Bragg. In the stroller is some sort of speaker, amplifying sound both he and the child can live with. Taken together, the Empire has invaded: U.S. Army, the State of North Carolina, Electricity, and the Rockefellers converge. These disruptions, I think, will prevent any sort of spiritual transformation, not to mention the occasional percussion of machine gun and single shot fire back across the highway. I leave the painted rock of "A Million Dreams" on the fence.

More empires.

From here, I continue walking, finding side paths that I hope circle back in some way to the park entrance. One is blocked off, but I take the path anyway, first stumbling on a beautiful array of pines before two separate dead ends where the trails run directly in to Bragg property.

I make my way back to one of the main trails, a loop the park ranger identified, determined to revisit the burned area I saw before, this time from the other side. The burned forest is acres of land. I find what I'm looking for a few hundred years down this path and veer my steps straight into the blackened area. I stumble among partly burned brush, downed trees, and still smoldering tree trunks or holes in the ground.

Several dozen yards into the wasteland, there's another of these
smoldering places.

It produces that lovely, bitter smell of burning wood. As I approach it, my feet warm in response to the heated ground around the hole. It's never quite uncomfortable but certainly unexpected.

My brain turns to stories of Moses and burning bushes. The ground I stand on is certainly holey; maybe it's holy, too.

The smell is right, a natural incense. The ground is warm. The forest is in transformation. The space is relatively clear. It's here where I'll do my work. A few feet away, just downwind from the smoldering hole and in the shadow of a bulky pine, I sit down and unpack my objects, which now includes a set of Bose earbuds, and pour my tea. I'm reminded that in Buddhist practice, it is common to expose objects like mala beads and even whole spaces to smoke. It's a way of cleansing them from harmful spirits and intents. In certain Christian churches, they cense the altars and communion elements, signifying holy presence. This space should be good to go.

Shrines and such.

The incense I've brought soon mixes with acrid smoke of the smoldering hole a few feet away. I turn to consult Jodorowsky and LeValley, settling first on his essay on space, then next on a meditation he provides that looks both inward and outward, inviting me to dissolve the distinctions between myself and the cosmos. I meditate in some silence. There are occasional crackles of something, and here and there the sound of an insect. The gunfire persists. I drink my tea. There is no one here.

After a while, still uncertain of whether I'm doing whatever it is I've invented here quite right, I decide to experiment, drowning out the gunfire with my earbuds. I flip to an app called "Shaman Magic," which plays looping drum sequences, supposedly authentic, and offers to mix in nature sounds like that of thunderstorms or forests. I skip the nature sounds and go straight to the drums. I turn the volume up and, after a moment, lie down and close my eyes. The smoke is still there, the sun bright and hot as I drape my ballcap over my face. At some point over the next few minutes, I become anxious as I feel like maybe I'm being watched and sneak a peek out from under my cap. Nothing. There is no one here. The anxiety returns after I close my eyes, but this time, I try to let it go. After a while, the drum loop ends and I stay on my back, letting the sounds of the natural world creep back in.

Both before and after the drums, I notice, nearby, an odd clicking coming from somewhere. It's probably an insect, but certainly one that I'm not sure I've heard. It doesn't rise to the music of a cricket, in my view. I decide to try to record it before the drumming meditation, but as soon as I open the recorder app on my phone, the sound dies almost on cue. After the drumming meditation, the clicking has returned and I'm able to get a few seconds recorded before I decide to track it down. I turn my head to listen for it behind me, but now it seems in front of me, coming almost from the base of the bulky pine, and I can't locate the source. Before my turn with the drums, I'm focusing on my breath and the clicking reminds me of a heartbeat or a drum itself, some creature of the natural world tapping me into a meditative trance.

In that trancelike state, one I've come to recognize in meditation and occasionally at TBC as a sort of refreshing, energized mental state where I feel like I'm resident in my body, I pack up, return to the clicking tree, touch it, and move along through the burned forest for over an hour, letting my mind use cues to tell me where to go. This tree makes me think I should go that way. That landmark is oddly beautiful. This downed tree points me in a direction. There are five or so smoldering places along the way. It is hot. I see, at my feet and really all over the place, tiny white butterflies with wings no bigger than a dime.

I land back on the sandy path some time later, and I'm covered with soot, more or less head to toe. I'm sweaty and it's a long enough walk back. This time, the forest, the part unburned, is on my right, and the crush of deciduous leaves pushes forth from the green space. The leaves belie the species, one of which is a sweetgum. Further ahead in the parking lot, a Bragg soldier, dressed in running gear, emerges from his SUV. The license plate is from Missouri. He's here from there most recently, transferred from Ft. Leonard Wood. A few minutes' drive away, I'm at a local barbecue joint trying to get my blood sugar up, and the folks at a table across the room are talking about the Ozarks, a mountain range in Missouri.

These, to me, are signs. I'm from Missouri, spent countless summers of my youth in the Ozark mountains, whether dashing through rippling creeks and rivers not unlike the French Broad while fishing with my grandfather or trail-walking with my parents and siblings, collecting rocks. In the front yard of my grandparents' house in Kansas City is a sweetgum tree, which seasonally drops spiny balls containing seeds they called gumballs. They hurt on bare feet, and I used to collect them, too. My father, a traveling Baptist pastor and teacher at one point, crisscrossed the State of Missouri with us kids in tow, visiting state parks and barbecue joints in equal measure. Kansas City barbecue, in particular, is a reminder of growing up. So are gumballs, as we called them, and license plates, and Ozarks. Perhaps these things present themselves to me because I've suggested, as De Martino might observe, that they do: I'm looking for signs and meaning. After all, it's not uncommon for someone from Fayetteville to encounter anyone from somewhere else. The Army draws people from everywhere to serve here. Or perhaps after an afternoon spent in the symbolic, the liveliness of green versus the black of death, the blending of my narrative and empirical cues to craft a story or experience, I'm inclined to see these coincidences as something more than they are. Or perhaps the cosmos has something to say to me, thinly, after a morning of having engaged it intently.

After eating, I pop over to a gas station to fill my fuel tank, and on a whim, I test the magic on a couple of lottery tickets. No luck. Maybe the material world can create a magic opening, a thin place, but the magic and the spiritual doesn't want to be used for such crass purposes.

I don't think my trip to Carver's Creek was a thin place experience, or especially sacred, as much as it was me writing a neat story to collect and describe a series of phenomena in an attempt to make sense of my world on the heels of a graduate course in shamanism and another in personal identity. For a fleeting moment, I wondered if the presence I experienced during the drumming or the source of the clicking might be a kind of spirit helper in Bran's terms.

Even now, I'm not entirely sure TBC is a thin place, either. Maybe Bushi is a thin person, or maybe Buddhist practice invites thin experiences. When I was younger and not dashing about Missouri in the summer, my family vacationed every so often in North Carolina, coming across Thomasville to visit friends in Asheboro before we moved on to the beaches of the coast. We'd spend a few days in Asheboro and the nearby town of Seagrove, hardly a town at all but home to several dozen potteries that cropped up in the middle of the twentieth century. The potters like Seagrove's particular brand of clay, and a community formed around that element. As a child, we'd wander, my hands behind my back, through stores full of colorfully glazed plates and coffee cups, vases and pitchers and figurines, all hand made. If I take the scenic route, I can pass through Seagrove on my way to or from TBC. That scenic route also runs right over the Uhwarrie river and gives me a glimpse of the old Uhwarrie mountain range, worn and round-topped like the Ozarks. Perhaps it is my own story and history that makes TBC a thin place. Perhaps it is my identity as a Christian and a Shakespeare scholar and practitioner that makes St. Bart's thin, and my experience is a sort of nostalgic reconstruction of my psychological and emotional past spent among rocks. Maybe my commute to TBC is a kind of psychomagic. I like the way Bushi and Mike Morrell think, though, and I wonder if the distinctions matter. The magic is working, maybe. Perhaps everything is thin if we look at it.

A couple of days later, I'm sharing some of my photos of the charred forest and someone points me to a recent state NPR story on forest management in and around Carver's Creek. It turns out the site of the controlled burn is the result of a highly recognized collaboration between the state, biologists, and Fort Bragg meant to save one of the rarest butterflies in the world, the St. Francis Satyr. The Army's artillery exercises ignite the fires necessary for these controlled burns to return the land to something habitable to the butterflies, empire and nature working together to restore the beings meant to live there.[27] The trauma of the artillery fire, and perhaps of the gunfire at the Clay Target Center, and of personal and theatrical dramas like bipolar disorder and depression, clear out the thick brush, literal and symbolic, both transforming the material world and enabling transformation of the caterpillar or the person cocooned. And wherever this happens, the thing becomes thin.

Imagination

"If you've ever been in the vicinity of the sacred—ever brushed against the holy—you retain it more in your bones than in your head; and if you haven't, no description of the experience will ever be satisfactory." – Daniel Taylor, *In Search of Sacred Places*

A core part of my journey included painting as a personal practice, and the creation of one work in particular. If and when I stretch to talk about this painting, so much of what I have to say involves communication and meaning that is beyond language. I can talk about the painting in some ways: my mother is a painter and I've been somewhat of a hobbyist, dabbling on canvases from time to time, or doing scenic painting for the plays I've been involved in over the years.

Aphrodite?
Jacob French

I chose to paint inspired by Jung's work with what he terms "Active Imagination," a kind of dreaming via paintbrush, where you just sort of let your mind and body do the work and see what happens. I can say this is also why I don't have stop motion or process photos of the thing, because worrying about that or interrupting the active dreaming would move the work out of the unconscious and into the empiricist approach that it is not. I can say that after doing the painting and engaging in Active Imagination, I felt both strangely alive and somewhat shamed—like it wasn't enough to be "real" work. But, as others viewed my work, the Jungian archetypes in my work became apparent - a red-haired Aphrodite, a rising sun in darkness, a transformative being in a chaotic space. And those observations seem like my story.

The plane of imagination.
Jacob French

This personal practice and deep exploration gave me a chance to spend time in my own tomb, my own life, my own story, but with a presentness of mind that was lacking prior to this. I consider this work to be part of my emerging recovery and reconstruction, but not an end. A couple years' stint in a kind of rehab, perhaps, but not the end of the process.

Fairy Tale Endings

I created a fairy garden that represents, in rock, soil, moss, and plant, among other things, a fairy tale place in my life. I have never built a fairy garden and might have otherwise had no reason to, save that it is a place where a bit of memory is contained, tangibly and practically.

The garden with a little bonfire.

A while back, I was experiencing big time trauma. I was not as alert to it then as I am now, and it was, for me, as shocking as any fairy tale only real, there, in my body. The trauma was deeply psychological in nature, and of course it affected all my relationships as I was both traumatized and traumatizing as I enacted daily what I have come to learn were stories I have told myself since my youth. These were stories deeply embedded with things like shame, embarrassment, and grief, and were mostly told alone, in my head and body, either out of habit (in the case of my mind) or instinct (in the case of my body). I found myself on a sofa across from a woman I'll call Monica, a therapist, whose first session with me involved her writing furiously on a whiteboard the basics of the sympathetic and parasympathetic nervous systems, and a quick breakdown of polyvagal theory. She explained that my body—the whole thing, not just the mind—stores trauma, calling up the very real responses it has had to prior threats. Think of this like your body engaging in a sort of primordial fight, flight, freeze, or fawn response, but at everything. If you are *in* trauma, as I was, it is almost as though your body is in control of you instead of the other way around: the body tells you it is under threat, almost constantly. Monica's role, then, was to help to train my body and brain to tell themselves a different story.

I began a months-long process to do just that: tell myself a different story through things called processing and a couple really odd practices such as EMDR, which stands for Eye Movement

Desensitization and Reprocessing, and tapping. At the time, I called these practices "magic" to my friends. The basic idea is that you recall a stressful situation, and your body starts to set itself off—engaging that fight or flight response. Then a magician-therapist steps in and either makes you follow her fingers with your eyes or taps you lightly on the hands or legs while you are recalling a traumatic event and your body is going haywire. The result of this EMDR or tapping work is essentially that your brain scrambles the signal sent to your body, making fuzzy the mental image that was setting your body off with a story of threat. The techniques intentionally confuse the existing memory and my judgments about it, actually replacing one story with another, nearly opposite story, transforming the body's reaction in turn. When I say magic, I mean it. Within days of a given session, images and events that had occupied me for months or years just sort of went away. I still think about them, but my body tells a different story.

Before my work with Monica began in EMDR and tapping, we worked on some strategies for calming my nervous system in case I was in session or experienced what is called "flooding," or acute flashbacks that can occur for days after a session. One of those strategies was to create what Monica called a "calm, safe place." For almost the length of an entire session, she led me through an exercise to visualize a place that I could go to in my mind that would help to calm me. The session involved closing my eyes as Monica played some calming music and then asked me a series of questions that increased in specificity and enabled me to essentially invent a little world for myself, a retreat to which I could escape. At first, I was in a field, grassy with flowers and snow-capped mountains in the background. I walked to the edge of a forest beyond. I entered the forest. I found a little glade, surrounded by pine trees, with a trickling brook wandering through it. Monica turned on the sounds of a running stream. As her questions persisted, in my mind materialized a caravan wagon, lit brilliantly inside with lanterns and adorned with pillows and carpets. Outside the wagon was a place for a fire, and some benches for seating. Monica turned on the sound of a crackling fire. Over the next few moments, I was asked about every inch of the space, made to articulate every detail I could. Later, in session, I might have to go back, and the detail moved our work from abstraction to mental reality. What I did not realize at the time was how much this little mental retreat—"The Glade," we called it—was built on the archetypes found in the fairy tale tradition, romantic as they are sometimes wont to be. A little lodging in the woods, enshrouded in mystery, where possibility happens. But even as I've come to appreciate that, more intriguing for me is the way in which The Glade, EMDR, and tapping serve not only as a kind of fairy tale writing in which new worlds and endings are forged from the trauma of real life but also as a kind of contemporary magic.

Fairy tales took shape around campfires and cookstoves. Deep in them, they are stories of trauma, they are about rifts in families emerging from the deaths of mothers in childbirth, the detachment experienced by women and children from fathers who labored far afield, the uncertain allegiance and economic displacement threatened by the presence of families mixed by remarriage, or the problem of inheritance.[28] In these stories, the trauma bears itself out largely in the bodies of women and children. Bodies are chopped up, cooked, poisoned, eaten, or buried. Some of these traumas are meant to be taken literally, but most are emblems of the mental and emotional traumas a modern therapist might understand as a condition of the mind informed by the traumatized condition of the body.

Fairy tales use magic and fantasy as a means of transgressing the natural way of things, like re-growing limbs or resurrecting bodies, stitching on heads, splitting open wolves to reveal whole persons, or restoring families. This magic is the same magic of bonfire experiences – disorienting and disobedient – as it pursues the unexpected, the surprising, and the strange. This transgression is a kind of trauma reversal, a means of breaking or bending the rules of nature in the way that these characters' bodies and minds break. In reshaping the world and its possibilities, the fairy tale processes trauma by transforming the world to match, poetically, the brokenness of the traumatized character. As we encounter fairy tales, it is less important that the world is transformed than it is that our character imagines that possibility.

Such transformation is possible at the level of community – in the corporate body. Fairy tales remind us regularly of belonging. In some takes, there is a sense that each group is an organism unto itself, whether it be a family, a laboring village, a kingdom, or the animal communities of the forest and field. Fairy tales center on relationships of belonging. The tales themselves create perhaps an ultimate form of community across time and space as they teach morals and virtues and character. The invitation here is that community — and specifically the community that emerges around the experience of stories — is a means of processing trauma, like a diaspora of emotion spread across the Jewish people, or the arresting boredom of being a housewife dispersed among a menagerie of animal companions.[29]

We are reminded here, of course, that these communities, these corporate bodies, can and do experience trauma, too. Fairy tale scholars point us to the social, collective trauma encountered as these stories emerged in the oral tradition, from the abandonment of children, to abusive men, to the destitution experienced by daughters and wives whose fathers' and husbands' absences or deaths destabilized whole households. Others see this trauma playing out in families and across human development, especially in childhood and adolescence. Where some deal in time (i.e., human development), scholar Donald Haase sees fairy tales as offering the *space* for meting out traumas in a safe, imagined place. He suggests that those who experience traumatic "circumstances might have used the fairy tale as a device to interpret their surroundings and as a psychological survival tool to transform their environment into a hopeful utopian space, a reconstituted home."[30] To me, this sounds like the calm, safe space Monica fostered for me – and its physical reputation in my little fairy garden.

All of these suggest that stories emerge as a way of processing that trauma in communal terms. It is not only important, therefore, that we tell and hear stories that allow us to reshape the world. It is important that we enact them in the new corpuses made up in the narrative communities these tales are meant to serve. In fact, it is because we are processing these communal traumas and these individual, personal traumas that we see stories about bodily trauma emerge in our stories. Narratively speaking, violent dismemberment, as an example, stands in for these other traumas, and the stories themselves become something of a safe place for the working out of our grief and, if you will, post-traumatic stress — in poetic terms. The fairy tale model is a memory-making device, not unlike my fairy garden, helping to "facilitate recall" in the minds and bodies of the hearers, allowing them "to store, remember, and reproduce the plot of the tale and change it to fit their experiences."[31] This work is ultimately about transformation, as "people have always wanted to improve and/or change their personal status or have sought magical intervention on their behalf."[32]

In this way, fairy tales and fairy gardens may be—with the right intent behind them—places where traumas are buried, like brothers, with the hope of a transformation or resurrection story following magically behind.

* * *

A post-script on fairy tale gardens. I mentioned much earlier that I'd gotten to move into a new office and redesign it. As I write, I'm currently looking at a version of the Glade. There are tapestries of trees hung all around. One features a brightly burning campfire against the backdrop of the Aurora Borealis. I have some of those orange lights that flicker like torches, a soft green chair and a green rug like grass. Sometimes I play the sounds of water. It's work, so it isn't always a calm, safe space. It is, however, a real, live poem.

Part 3

Kindling

The Fire You're Already Burning

Many of the crises I've described in these pages are part of a story I wasn't happy with having written, as well as part of a story in which I no longer found meaning. I think that's probably another way of saying I was in deconstruction. The words were still there, but no longer made sense together. The body was still there, but the character was not. I mean that as thoroughly as I possibly can: I was in a character crisis. The process of Controlled Burning is simply to take the danger of the fire and repurpose it for good. While a wild-fire can annihilate an ecosystem, a controlled burn can make it come alive in new and more sustainable ways.

Reconstruction is about re-authoring one's story, to some degree. I mean that in all the ways that the self-help industry has made that notion popular in the last few generations, but I also mean it in much more practical terms. As a professional storyteller for all of my adult life, I have the skills to weave magical and moving and transformative tales of wonder and delight. I've just never been in those tales myself. Directors and many other artists are persistent and insistent outsiders in this regard, not merely loners. We're in the room, like priests. And like priests, or like professors or like teachers, we are involved in a unique way. We are not the audience. Our perspective is different and can even feel foreign and detached when laid alongside that of other observers. Our experience is uncommon. I think I mostly considered that to be an alienating and dispiriting factor for most of my life. It shouldn't be. Like priests and shamans and preachers and storytellers and bonfire experiences, we are even more closely involved than most everyone else. And it is good to be weird. We owe it to each other to be different. And so what I see for myself is continuing a life with all of that in mind, with a special blessing on my head. What was a curse — a fiery, alienating, traumatic, destructive force — can be inverted and transformed into blessing. You just have to burn the right stuff.

Let me return to something I said earlier: burning is a feature of a bonfire, not a flaw. There are people who will argue with you about that, who will quibble over the temperature of the thing, who will wring their hands over errant sparks and hot knuckles. There are those who will stand resentfully at the back of the party and accuse the storytellers of oversharing. There are those who will micromanage the Controlled Burn rather than just manage it. A bonfire does not care about these things – not even the metaphorical kind. This is its grace, burning up needless anxiety and obedient thinking, and it is good. The job is to burn. The long bet of this book is that you are burning or ready to burn – in good, necessary, magical ways.

Our little bonfire of a book here is soon to fade into embers. What I hope to leave you with is enough kindling and spark from the fire I've burned here so that you can start your own, and so you can gather with me over time in a kind of campfire community. What follows are some types of "Kindling" – fire-starting tips for getting your own Bonfire Experience going.

Gathering

Let's get practical for a moment. To have bonfires, you have to gather two things: the stuff you want to burn and the people who are going to hang out. Hopefully the Burning Questions below will help you gather some stuff to burn. I urge you to take those questions and let them do their work, serving as a kind of kindling or inspiration or Muse for you as you work on them. There is, of course, plenty more stuff to gather that's worthy of burning – especially in your story. There's trauma. There's drama. There's damage to manage. Bring that stuff, too. I heartily invite you to join me in the mixing of literal and metaphorical here. Sometimes the symbol of an intangible, ineffable concept can be as powerful as those concepts. This is an invitation to play with fire. Here are some ideas to get your fire started:

- The nightgown your mother wore the night she discovered her own mother died
- The missing pages of your relationship with your father
- The hope chest your one-time fiance gave you before they broke things off
- The budget sheets you put together for a dream that never came to fruition
- The stacks and stacks of contracts and other broken promises you've accumulated

- The scripts of plays for which there is no longer a role for you
- The diary of all your deep secrets
- The leftovers from your favorite meal
- The leaves you've raked up to get ready for a party

As for people to gather, I hope that when you bring your stuff to burn, you will do it with the full support of professionals – licensed mental health and massage therapists (not kidding!), physicians, professors, and personal trainers, ministers who know what they're doing, and others who know what Controlled and Uncontrolled Burning are, even if they use their own frameworks for understanding those things. I hope you'll gather literally with bodies of people – theatre companies or community organizations, civic or religious groups, folks who show up regularly to the bar or the river. When you gather, gather with actual bodies. Online communities like those for gamers can be great, but they are rarely a substitute for the magic that happens when bodies move, touch, and sense out there in the world.[33] I also hope you'll start your own parties when you can, like gathering wood for a new fire.

To have bonfires, you have to gather the stuff and gather the people, but you also have to have a *gathering*: an intentional, specific, delightful, well-designed, disorienting event that creates a shared experience and facilitates storytelling – even and especially a story about the event itself. "I don't know how to describe it," you might say, "but what happened last night at the party was magical. One of the best nights of my life." This is what we're after. I hasten to add that I'm not just talking about a single event here, but an ongoing way of gathering that keeps the fire going. That could be an event, but can also be a life on fire in the right way.

Gathering people is creating relationships. At the core of that word is the word *relate* and it means *to tell*. Meaningful relationships begin with a shared story or a shared experience. You can have all the theatre companies and churches and friends in the world, but if there is no gathering, no collective story, there is no bonfire experience. I know this because at times in my life I've shown up to groups of people and there is no fire: the workplace when it is deadly, the uninspired organization, the cold relationship. People alone do not magic make.

Gathering people is creating communion. Earlier on, I told you that this wasn't a religious book, and it still isn't. I'm using communion here to mean what happens when we operate together in our spirits. When we are on fire together. When there's a common buzz or collective energy. When the party is great. When the magic happens. See, shared stories are good – but it is the kind of shared story, the nature of the experience that makes the Deep Work happen. It is not just about how your day went or what happened one time at summer camp. It is not a story with a punchline. Instead, it is about who and how you are: not smoke, but fire.

On gathering: I have perhaps the world's most insistent "make it work" mentality. I believe some of the best Bonfires are made from a kind of scrappy resourcefulness that says, simply, *use what you have*. I'm a true believer in the necessity of imagination in making magic happen – from a trauma-informed transformation to a beautiful bonfire. You don't need your A-list guests, you need the person standing in front of you. You don't need brand-name marshmallows, you need the stale ones left over from Thanksgiving. You don't need craft beer, you need the whispers of whiskey in the bottle at the back of the cabinet. In the theatre, I make rooms with cheap colored lighting and drapey fabric that I've accumulated over the years. In the classroom, I try to start with the willing learners I have before me. Having said all this, I arrived at this part of the book weeks ago and absolutely did not know what to do. Driven by the need for a "proper," "inspirational" ending, I ran through dozens of options in my head – where every idea came up short. And then I remembered what my panic obscured: to use what I have. And so I stopped writing and instead celebrated Thanksgiving with my family. I held a few little backyard bonfires with my wife while the neighborhood dogs barked encouragingly. I sang in a Christmas concert with my friends. I went to a business meeting *that actually moved me to tears in a good way*. I traveled for Christmas. I went to an amazing conference with Shakespeare people. I let these things do their work. And I let my deadlines pass.

It was on the first day of the conference that I wrote the end of this book in my head while participating in a truly transformative Bonfire Experience with folks who were mostly strangers at that point. The day before, I woke up at 1:30 in the morning. to drive to the airport, took two planes and a cab to get to the conference hotel in Nassau, Bahamas, and I did what I always do when I arrive in a new place, which is to walk over as many square inches as possible. While exploring, I ate the strangest food I could find – in this case some octopus – and dirtied the bottom cuffs of my trousers with sand and saltwater. The next morning, I woke up at 4:30 in the morning to attend Nassau's Junkanoo Festival, a massive New Year's street parade that begins at midnight and is still – believe me – roaring in the early hours. With my fellow conference attendees, I wandered through back streets watching parade entries consisting of blaring horns and buzzing drums, wild costumes, and enormous, cartoonish floats. After several blocks, we arrived at the main square, where hundreds of people gathered on bleachers to watch the entries. As the sun came up, we bleary-eyed folks witnessed a few of the remaining entries in the parade. While all were lively and full of spectacle, the final one was from another world. The entry was *hundreds* of people – musicians, dancers, costumed folks wearing entire set pieces, floats. The sound was, without question, the loud-est, most sustained sound I've ever heard in my life. It was pure vibration, pure life.

An hour later, after a breakfast of stew fish and orange juice, I found myself seated on a folding chair in a circle with a few dozen other conferees in the conference host's black box theatre for a session called "Speak What We Feel: Shakespeare and Trauma Treatment."[34] It is here where the Bonfire Experience really started to burn. I want to put you in that room for a moment:

At first, we are invited just to sit, breathe, and look at each other in the room. The invitation is to really take folks in, these strangers (and new friends), and to assess when we felt we had to change our behavior in response to someone else – to notice when we were performing for others or accepting others and ourselves on equal terms. We also notice how funny and judge-y we all get when someone arrives a bit late. "Notice that," is the invitation. "Try to move it to a neutral, nonjudgmental place. The invitation is also to slow down, and the contrast of this quiet, reflective space on the heels of the raucous Junkanoo Festival could not have been starker. This feels like a cousin of Buddhism and a close friend of therapy. I'm into it.

The session leaders are Stephan Wolfert and Dawn Stern, the husband and wife team that do the work of DE-CRUIT, an organization that uses Shakespeare in deep, science- and research-based work with veterans, Gold Star families, and others who've experienced significant trauma.[35] Stephan is an Army veteran himself, who "used to jump out of planes," he says. My ears immediately perk up at this – my home in Fayetteville, North Carolina, sees a lot of Army folks jumping out of planes, and a lot of people in trauma.

Stephan and Dawn spend the next three hours guiding us through a host of techniques, from breathing exercises and what they call "rituals of recovery" to journaling to an inventory of embodied feelings of self,[36] and, ultimately, reading a Shakespeare speech out loud. This reading – which a few people demonstrate in the room – is Deep Work, where the person first reads their journal entry and then reads the speech *as if it is their words*. Everyone is in tune with each other. We're witnessing people come into themselves and really share something fully human, fully alive. It's hard for me to capture in words what happens – but it is magical, transformative, the real deal. We begin to know each other.

Both Stephan and Dawn – and, as it turns out, almost everyone in that room – are on fire. While both are incredibly charismatic – as is almost everyone in this room of performers and artists – the fire in their work burns hot and deep. You can tell they're not merely experienced, having done this work perhaps now thousands of times, but that they're *here*, present, listening, noticing, and with us. They have gathered themselves and their stories and their resources and all of us, and a Bonfire Experience happens. There are few dry eyes by the time we're done, but that isn't really the point. This isn't meant to be a "mountaintop" experience of emotional manipulation. In fact, much of what happens is invited, as in the Buddhist tradition, to be aware of emotions but not compelled by them. A major difference between the mountaintop and the Bonfire is that the former is about attaining (as in new heights from which we will inevitably have to descend) and the latter is about discovering, opening, and sharing regardless of the ascending or descending nature of our lives. So much of Dawn and Stephan's work is about the *science* of trauma, recovery, and human behavior that they land for me much less like the actors they are and much more like the social workers I know. Around the room, I see the performers I knew were there, but I also find managing and executive directors, board members, lawyers, and a lovely person with a career in quantitative analytics. His story is there, too.

As I think about this Nassau morning some weeks on, I'm reminded of something I said earlier: what it takes to create such bonfire experiences:

- *Physically remove yourself from the current place.* Travel to the Bahamas works, I have to tell you, but so does moving through the streets, and from the streets onto the patio and from the patio into the little black room. Each shift is an opportunity to experience new and different fires.
- *Shape the new space in a meaningful way.* At Junkanoo, the space was shaped for me. In the black box of the Dundas Centre for the Performing Arts, the circle of chairs was a space I recognized as familiar after years in the theatre and elsewhere. Everything in this experience was shaped in space and with intention.

- *Immerse yourself in the new experience.* Junkanoo: wild, buzzing, energetic, colorful. Workshop: quiet, reflective, committed, fully aware of each other and ourselves.
- *Sit.* Junkanoo bleachers: anticipatory, celebratory space that vibrated underneath us and prompted us to enjoy what's next. Workshop: folding chairs and perfunctory theatre seating, open orientation, close connection to the people next to and across from us.
- *Burn.* Junkanoo: all-consuming, sensory, hot, lit, spectacular, crackling. Workshop: internal heat, inspiring, communal, truly warm. Both: transforming.
- *Tell stories.* Junkanoo: stories new to me, and a new story I can share. Workshop: deep stories developed in journaling and shared in speeches, stories of recovery shared by Stephan and Dawn, my story here.
- And I'll add one more here: *Use what you have.* Junkanoo: cardboard, paint, craft store decorations, personal musical instruments, and a lot of other human beings. Workshop: body, breath, experience, text.

  Perhaps it's easy for me to backwards engineer my experience at the conference and force it to fit my Bonfire definition. It is also easy for me to champion wonderful experiences set in paradise with hundreds of dollars in airfare and hotel stays and privilege behind them. What I hope gives *you* hope in my story here is that I found what I was looking for in these moments because they're extensions of my life, work, and interests. You'll have your own versions that happen over coffee and business calls if those things are what you have to play with. Again, that's easy for me to say. So let me give you another quick example, decidedly less exotic than a Bahamian Shakespeare adventure: school pickup with my kids.

- *Physically remove yourself from the current place.* I've driven a bright yellow truck for years. I pick up my daughter from high school, and we talk about a short story they read in class today by a Japanese author, Haruki Murakami. We are moving, letting the space of the town and the distance from that classroom inform us. We pick up my son from his school a few miles away. We learn about his affinity for recess. We travel home. There is a lot of sameness in this kind of ritual travel, but there's great possibility in these transitional, liminal spaces.
- *Shape the new space in a meaningful way.* My habit is listening to NPR. My daughter's habit is popping their headphones in. My son's habit is a quick doze. We can change the space of these moments by way of a car wash, a stop at the video game store (of which they are both fans), by the playing of U2's *40* on the truck's stereo, or visiting Starbucks.
- *Immerse yourself in the new experience.* Seriously, the car-wash works a kind of magic. Literal immersion. Car baptism. Something happens in the body.
- *Sit.* We are seated, receiving stories about the day, anticipating the future, in a state of "not yet," weary but eager.
- *Burn.* When we're intentional, we can dig into the stories under the story, the joy under the exhaustion of the day. I can learn who these people are and they can learn me – not what we did that day, but who we are. This is burning.
- *Tell stories.* You get it.
- *Use what you have.* A cramped yellow truck that smells of pipe smoke (and sometimes contains pipe smoke – another kind of burn and sensory experience). A Spotify account. A car wash coupon. Caffeine.

I'll be the first and loudest to tell you that I'm not the most present father. My default is to run all day, every day, and my life is often an endless state of rehearsal. I've been delighted in recent years to have my kids join me at rehearsals and in the creative work, and even more delighted to see them undertake their own creative lives that are and are not like mine. Add to my lack of presence a season of trauma, depression, withdrawal, and darkness to which my kids were both primary witnesses. I remember days when I was sunk so far into the recliner in flight or freeze mode that I might as well have become the furniture itself. I likewise remember days when I was so ablaze with uncontrolled, raging energy that I might have combusted right on the spot. One day, in the middle of all this, I came home late from one rehearsal or performance or another and found a circle of Post-It hearts on my door that said, "We Love You, Daddy." That was a Bonfire Experience, too. They knew my story enough that I didn't have to tell it – I was showing it and they were attending to it, metabolizing it, and transforming it into something new. Since that time, I try to remind myself that a long-burning Bonfire Experience has to have everyone contributing to make the moments work – my kids are not responsible for sustaining me as a person. But they did that time, just as we take turns telling stories or move in and out of the light around the fire.

Fire Insurance

I can't leave you without talking about the theatre in all this – and its practical offerings to the idea of Controlled Burning.

Bonfires – the corporate, communal ones we're dealing with here – are a kind of theatre. There's a flat, empty space we fill with objects, bodies, and light. There's scenery of one sort or another. There's sound, from the crackle of the wood to the chirping of crickets to the bad (or good) music blaring from someone's stereo to the hum of humans chatting away. There are stories. There are little performances, dances from light to darkness and from warmth to cool, the spinning of marshmallows and hotdogs on sticks – these being props, of course. There are costumes of flannel and floral dresses, poofy jackets and polo shirts, overdressed and overworn. Together, these things make a place where, as in theatre, anything is possible. Performance and religious scholars, anthropologists, and others who specialize in everything from making plays to studying rituals to examining how cultures treat transitions from adolescence to adulthood call such things *liminal spaces*. Liminal spaces are the *thresholds* – the transitional, transformational places and moments – between where we've come from and where we've not yet arrived. The Bonfire is a liminal experience in time and space where expectation rules, where we are not fully shaped, and from which we will emerge in a new state, changed. We come out of the Bonfire Experience as mutants. In the theatre, we call some of the mutants at the center of the experience actors, and their charge is to mutate themselves – to present characters and stories that are *not* their own – so that we, the audience, may be mutated.

Certain kinds of theatre – including most of the ones I'm involved with – are built around what I've come to call "insurance policies."[37] These practices are designed to make the magic and transformation of a given production happen, even when something goes wrong or when maybe the audience just isn't feeling it tonight or when something falls short of our expectation. In many ways, these *insurance policies* are really *assurance practices* – confidence-building guarantees for a good time at the play and true transformation as we emerge from the liminal space and time where and when the play happens. Some of these practices are innate to all theatre and Bonfire Experiences, while many emerge as peculiar, even esoteric. What I've found is that working with and refining these insurance policies in all kinds of settings helps channel the magic we're looking for. They're together an on-ramp for the transformational journey, or a set of spells, or a kind of delight engine – bellows pumping to make the burn brighter and more beautiful. Despite these coming from my experience as a theatre and event maker, I've tried to situate these insurance policies in the rest of the world – and in the Bonfire metaphor. Here goes:

- *An Open, Compelling Invitation*: Everything begins with welcome – but a lot of folks will not gather just because they're welcome. They'll come because the invitation – whether it's a poster design, a text invite, an email, or your decorations – compels them to come. Lots of things can do this work, but I've found *beauty and earnestness are the best tools*. This is the act of not just opening the invitation, but taking folks by the (literal or metaphorical) hand. In theatre, an invitation could be a killer poster design, but it is more likely word of mouth, an exceptional photo of other humans, or friends who bring you along. In the world, it is these things, too.

- *Surprise/Intrigue*: Perhaps the number one thing they teach you in directing school is to *stay ahead of your audience.* You have to keep them leaning forward, in a near-constant state of delightful surprise. This means the experiences have to be interesting, real, authentic to you and to them, and crafted such that anything is possible. The surprises have to be good surprises. As soon as your audience is ahead of you, they're out: making grocery lists, running through all the things they have to do this week, or balancing their checkbooks in their heads. How do you do this? Make unexpected choices. Stay weird. If you're bored, they're bored. Much of this work is about healthy, non-sexual seduction – almost like flirting with the world and its people so that they become and stay interested, but without the darkside of manipulation.

- *Shared Light*: The light of a Bonfire Experience is *shared light, not spotlight*. We're talking about literal light and the "energy" of an experience. While we may all take turns standing closer or farther away from the central experience, the light is shared by all. Shared light should create a sense of equity and belonging. Playing with shared light also means learning that some folks will want the attention of a close seat and some will want to linger back and observe – and that this process can be managed as we sometimes throttle back our attention-seekers and quietly join and encourage our introverted and observer friends. Outside of events, shared light is about the give and take of energy where the mantra, *"It's not about you,"* rings politely in our ears.

- *Surrounded Space*: A Bonfire Experience is a circle; a Controlled Burn radiates outward. It is not like most theatres or places of worship or classrooms or workshops, where the "special" or "important" stuff – often led by specially-designated leaders – happens and others passively watch. In the theatre, we call such orientations "thrust" or "arena" staging, and the very act of these shifts makes it easier to *see other people's faces and bodies* and *to have our own faces and bodies seen* alongside whatever the central thing is – a fire, a story, a play, a conversation. As we look for Bonfire Experiences, we need a radial space of radical welcome that everyone can engage on their own terms, where hierarchies are weakened (if not broken altogether), and where we can all join the circle.
- *Simple Staging*: A lot of us party planning types drift into wanting big scenery, flashy lights, a killer sound system, fancy props, and cool special effects. A lot of humans just want things to look or feel "special." We think we have to travel to have special experiences. We have to make a big event. We have to decorate. A lot of the impulse behind these things is just insecurity, an anxiety to perform – to be seen as worthy. I'm here to tell you that a lot of these complexities get in the way. Bonfire Experiences are about *simple human connection, story making, and the stripping away of the "extra"* rather than the layering on of it.
- *Doubling*: In theatre, doubling is the idea that one actor plays more than one part. The joy of this is that we get to see them pretend in multiple ways – to literally see them in different roles. Powerful things happen when we see others outside of their usual roles, undone, hair down, relaxed, unbusinesslike – or whatever alternate or even contradictory role might emerge. "I didn't know you played guitar," I might say to

Bryan, my accountant acquaintance who tends to strike me as pretty buttoned-up. Doubling is about *seeing the multiplicity of each other's identities* at play – and to see the whole human in a different light.

- *A Backstage, Backyard View*: Bonfires are best when they allow us into the places we might not otherwise see. In the backyard, this is the space that is less guarded and manicured and staged than the front yard. In the theatre, this is the wing space or dressing rooms where we see the real, unvarnished things before they become the theatrical, showy, or "on" versions of themselves in front of an audience. This is where we *see the person, not the personality* – the human being, not the character. A backstage/backyard feel is different, deeper – like being inside the cosmic joke, fully welcomed, aware of play and not-play.

- *Multiple Stakeholders*: Shakespeare's theatre company and peer companies of the region were run by a group of "Sharers" – literal shareholders in the company who put their money, labor, and expertise into a common enterprise. Everyone had skin in the game. There are a lot of theatre companies, non-profit organizations, studios, classrooms, families, and other settings that do this kind of multilateral "Sharing" work today. At the same time, this is not the way most companies or businesses work, and therefore not something many of us are familiar with. Having multiple stakeholders – true partners in the conversation, event, enterprise, play, meeting, relationship, Bonfire, and so on – is an act of radical welcome and a protest against the top-down nature of most of the rest of our lives. *Sharing enables everyone to be a leader and a follower simultaneously.* The common effort and equality of belonging makes us members of the organization, the organism that is humanity, and the Body of work we make together.

- *Comfort, Nostalgia, and Old Favorites*: Delight is, in part, about engaging the familiar – the rituals, memories, and habits where we take comfort. A Bonfire is powerful because so many things are familiar – the people, the sensory experience, the openness, the fire itself. Even the parts of the Bonfire experience are familiar – lighting the fire, the sky fading from twilight to darkness, the kinds of fireside fare we eat and drink, and so on. Storytelling, too, is an opportunity for us to recall the delights and pains of the past. When I work in theatre, I'm pursuing this insurance policy by selecting plays and songs and ways of making that call upon people's collective memory (say of childhood, a national or cultural or communal past, or a great playlist selection that folks might hear and know). Doing Shakespeare itself means playing with the nostalgia of that writer in our culture, high school classrooms, and memory. For me, a lot of my work in theatre is about recreating for others the best ten nights of my life, all of which have some things in common: warm cafe lights, soft, well-kept grass, a picnic blanket, a charcuterie board or Ploughman's Lunch, a pitcher of Pimm's Cup, live music, a charming play, and friends (including past girlfriends!), and family. Calling forth my own nostalgia like this and making it for others is a way of making new comforts, and new memories that become old favorites, like the families that come back to our performances again and again as they form their own traditions. Outside the world of theatre, *this work is about regenerating the delights of our past,* however those might manifest themselves, and *working to ensure comfort* for others – making a home.

- *New Work*: Delight is also about experiencing new adventures, departing from the expected, and deviating from the ritual. Creating new work (especially together with others) forges fresh ideas and plays with possibility and unpredictability as it hearkens back to the idea of surprise mentioned earlier. New work empowers those involved to do the rich, rewarding effort of making something from nothing. *New work should be balanced against and in tension with the comfortable, nostalgic, and familiar* – we need both old and new to play in concert with each other. In Bonfires, we need old friends and emerging ones and perfect strangers, the tried-and-true recipes alongside the recent ones we just read about, a favorite beer and a seasonal selection. New work is about finding the "now-ness," being alert to the potential of the present, and dealing with what is before us without too much longing for what isn't here any longer.

- *Difference/Weirdness/Idiosyncrasies*: Bonfires and Controlled Burns are different from everyday life. They change the landscape – literally. They have their own internal rules that don't clearly fit with the rest of the world. A Controlled Burn is about burning something to give something else life. This is weird, counterintuitive, even seductive. To be a fully realized human being, part of the work is in differentiating ourselves and our experiences. As an artist, I want to avoid being derivative – of leaning on (or stealing) other people's work rather than developing my own voice. Are we here to talk about the weather? The news? Real Housewives? Or are we here to embrace the wonderful strangeness of each other and our world? *Bonfire Experiences are made by cultivating the unusual.*

- *Casting – Earnest v. Polished Participants*: We keep returning to the idea of "peeling away" or revealing our authentic selves. This insurance policy suggests that our work is strongest when people aren't performing, polished, presentational, or uptight. Bonfires invite engagement with each other as human beings who have *shed the little lies of making things sound better than they are*, or having a clear punchline or moral at the end of our story. We're talking about the metaphorical difference between handmade and store-bought – crafted versus off-the-rack.

- *No Cell Phones*: No. Cell. Phones. So much of the currency of Controlled Burning and Bonfire experiences is simply in what we pay attention to: *here, now*.
- *Clear Cues*: If Bonfire Experiences and Controlled Burns are fundamentally about transformation, it helps if we signal this up front. *We can cue transformation in people by showing other simple things that have been transformed*. In the theatre I create, I look for simple, elemental design and environmental elements that we can transform like we want ourselves to be transformed. A swath of fabric can become an ocean, a projector screen, or a pool of blood. Wood can become a doorway, a plank, a staff, or a spear. A lantern can become a guidepost or a little magic trick for an on-stage wizard or witch. In the Bonfire metaphor, these cues are built into the fuel being burned, the marshmallows toasting, and so on. These cues tell us that transformation is possible – that *play* is possible. These cues prompt us to use our imaginations, which is where a lot of the bigger transformations have to take place first.
- *Enlivened Visuals*: Bonfires work because they're a spectacle. They're light contrasted against darkness. People on a stage or near a campfire are lit differently than they are by daylight, fluorescent work lights, or the incandescent lamps of home. The light moves and flickers. The costumes, too, are different.

The scenery is elevated. In some theatre design work, the whole place becomes an immersive environment. In outdoor theatre, all of nature is the scenery (same for a lot of literal fires). We must have cool things to look at that *activate our senses to see new worlds and ecosystems* that help to change our perspectives and inspire us.

- *Pleasant, Unusual Smells*: Here's another sensory insurance policy. Think burning wood, caramelizing sugars, the smell of Spring on the breeze. Think incense and bakeries. Think unfamiliar city streets and sweeping countryside. These smells rewire our brains, activate our bodies, and *prompt everything from nostalgia to curiosity*. Whether putting on a play or envisioning a Bonfire Experience, playing with smell is a quick path to getting the actual person – the human animal – to show up as themselves.

- *Sounds & Music*: Sensing a theme here (pun absolutely intended)? Whether chirping birds or crickets, crackling logs, a funky playlist, or clinking glasses, sound has the potential to transport us, change our moods, or even *cue our emotions into new and different states*. Being intentional with sound allows us to *hear things differently* – and this is the starting point for the Deep Work of listening.

- *Food & Drink*: Food and drink are more sensory insurance policies – but, for me, work on an even deeper level than some of the others mentioned. Unlike some of the other sensory practices, food and drink are also human needs – fundamental, foundational ones. I'm a big believer that no one can pay attention (let alone want to) if their basic needs are not met. Stomachs need to be fully and bodies hydrated. Food and drink are also the basis of a lot of understood human rituals of belonging, like meals, Communion, and so on. Food and drink *literally provide energy for the experience*, greasing the pathways for attention to be paid.

- *Excellent Craft*: In the theatre, there is no insurance policy that beats being really, really good at what you're doing. We want to see *humans operating at the highest level* – at the limits of their potential. Craft is the combination of person-hood, time, talent, technique, and work – a way of preparing for encounters with other people that will elevate your time together with them.
- *Chemistry*: Chemistry is the insurance policy that emerges from some of the others, the art and science of getting things just right, the energy created when things are burning well.

The thing about these insurance policies is that they work best when we stack them – when one of them insures another that ensures another and so on. "If I don't like the play," I might say, "then at least I'll be buzzed from the good beer." And if the beer is bad, I might like the music. And if the music is bad, I might like the company. And if the company is bad, I might like the story. And if the story isn't to my taste, I might like seeing it being made. And if that doesn't work, maybe there's at least something beautiful to look at. And so on. The chances of anyone making it through all the insurance policies and having a thoroughly miserable experience is small – not impossible, just small. Some folks are jerks. Sometimes our approach to any or all of these things is off. The point is that they make it more likely for people to discover and uncover who they are in each other's presence. These practices are kinds of The Work – and sorting out how they might work in your setting is part of The Work, too.

Burning Questions

Below is a list of questions that might help you light a spark towards your own bonfire experience or Controlled Burn.

This book is both a kind of Controlled Burn and a bit of a prescription for Controlled Burning that I hope will help you build your next fire. Spend some time writing your answers with a pen or pencil or graphic marker that feels great in your hand – that enables your best, most beautiful handwritten work – and *create* your answers. I say *create* because that includes analytical writing that might be familiar to most of us, but it can also include poetry, story, and visual expressions like doodling. Where you can, risk a venture into stories and visuals. You can always lean back on descriptive writing at any time.

Here are some questions I asked earlier. I invite you to use some of the blank pages at the end of the book to write your own responses to these questions.

- How big a fire is required?
- What are the environmental conditions needed to keep things safe and to promote new growth?
- How do we recognize when we're losing control of the fire? How do we manage the smoke?
- What protective equipment and methods do we need on hand?

- Who are we inviting to the bonfire and what should they bring?

  And here are some new ones:
- What does it mean to you to have a Bonfire Experience?
- Have you had an encounter(s) that felt like a Bonfire Experience?
- How do such experiences feel in your body or the bodies to which you belong?
- Reflect on that experience: what tools, resources, and communities were part of that experience? Can these serve as kindling for future bonfires?
- Can deep work take place in both thin and thick spaces?
- Can you create the environment conducive to Controlled Burning?
- What is it that is burning for you? What is it that needs burning?

Embers

Think of the following like a little worksheet or set of journal prompts based on some of the work I've shared earlier. Again, I invite you to use the blank pages at the end of this book to answer them.

- *Physically remove yourself from the current place.* How can you do this? What might physical removal look like if you can't really travel?
- *Shape the new space in a meaningful way.* What does shaping a space look like for you? What are your design inspirations? Where do you seek beauty that doesn't feel like you're just following someone else? What are some simple things you can do right now to make a tangible impact on your surroundings?
- *Immerse yourself in the new experience.* What does immersion feel like? What are the sounds, sights, smells, textures, tastes that truly overcome or transport you? How can you pay attention to these things? How can you use them to really surround yourself with awe and delight?
- *Sit.* Have you sat today – literally or metaphorically? When can you try this? Are you in a posture where you can receive from others? Are you open to receiving or is everything subject to an agenda? How can you shift toward the openness that sitting invites?

- *Burn.* What does The Work look like for you? How do you burn up the artifice and inauthenticity that surrounds us? What is the stuff in your life that ought to be cleared out with a good Controlled Burn? How do you burn now – how are you creating and clearing even now? Is it time for that fire to spread? Get under control?
- *Tell stories.* What is your story? Is it yours? Is it real? How can you weave it in with others' stories so that you and they are known fully?
- *Use what you have.* What do you have at hand? – knowledge, experiences, tools, resources, space, preferences, hopes, dreams?

Invitation

This is an invitation for you to light a fire – literal, metaphorical, Bonfire, Controlled Burn, campfire, you name it. As part of this invitation, I hope you'll rip out a few pages from the blank ones to follow – ones that, perhaps by now, you've filled with answers to some of the questions above. And I hope you'll use those pages to set fire to something special.

You've got things to burn. Let's get that fire started.

Burn this page.

Or this one.

Or any of these others.

JEREMY FIEBIG

JEREMY FIEBIG

JEREMY FIEBIG

JEREMY FIEBIG

DEFINITIONS ▌

- *Body*: Our own bodies, the bodies of our communities (i.e., a theatre company or a religious body or even a great class), and the bodies of the things we make, including bonfires.
- *Bonfire*: The actual thing burning. Could be oneself (metaphorically speaking, of course), a campfire, or a bonfire-like experience. Sometimes I use this image interchangeably as a concrete or embodied emblem for Controlled Burning.
- *Bonfire Experience*: A magical series of moments that happen when the space in our lives thins out, our senses and stories take over, and transformation happens. A Bonfire Experience can involve a literal bonfire or a metaphorical or symbolic one. A good play is a Bonfire Experience. A great meal, like a potluck, held in community, can be a Bonfire Experience. There are tons of other examples. Managed well, a Bonfire Experience can be sustained throughout one's life as an individual and as a community.
- *Controlled Burning*: the ongoing, necessary, destructive-and-creative work that is essential to bring about new growth – and my term for the art of the personal, communal, and ecological practices of burning the (metaphorical) undergrowth in the thick places in our lives. Sometimes used interchangeably with Deep Work or The Work.

- *Deep Work*: The Work under the work that makes the magic happen. Sometimes used interchangeably with Controlled Burning.
- *Embodied*: The quality of being in the body – one's own, a corporate one, or a physical object like a piece of art.
- *Magic*: The moments of ineffable, ethereal, and often indescribable transformation that happen in all kinds of bodies as a result of Controlled Burning, Bonfire Experiences, and The Work.
- *The Work*: See Deep Work.
- *Thick*: The nature of detritus around us – literal and metaphorical, physical, mental, spiritual, and relational – that has caught or easily catches fire.
- *Thin*: The quality of space, time, and spirit that is clear of thickness, eager for possibility, and ready for magic to happen.

END NOTES

1. Maslow's theory explores the motivation for human behavior. Lower and more foundational in the hierarchy are physiological ("body") needs for food, water, shelter, and so on. Higher needs can be met only when the more foundational needs are met. Higher needs are for things like belonging, esteem, and "self-actualization." For more on Abraham Maslow and his vaunted hierarchy, I humbly suggest a visit to your favorite search engine.

2. I touch on this in two of my "Firestarter" activities later in the book, but there's a lot that's fascinated me about Jung over the years, from archetypes to Active Imagination. If you have trouble getting started with Jung, I recommend Jung's more accessible disciple (of a sort), Joseph Campbell.

3. Indigenous people have been conducting controlled burns for time immemorial. The burning of grasses is described in Robin Wall Kimmerer's *Braiding Sweetgrass.*

4. This nugget is a direct quote from director and storyteller Guillermo del Toro, shared in an interview with NPR's Michel Martin, about his film *Pinocchio.* Interviewee Guillermo del Toro, "Guillermo del Toro Says Making His Pinocchio Was Healing," interview by Michel Martin, National Public Radio. https://www.npr.org/2022/12/10/1142099390/guillermo-del-toro-says-making-his-pinocchio-was-healing

5. Sort of. As with all things Jung, it's much more complicated than this, but you get the idea.

6. Mary DeMuth, *Thin Places: a Memoir* (Grand Rapids: Zondervan, 2010), 11.

7. Jeffrey Kripal, *Secret Body: Erotic and Esoteric Currents in the History of Religions* (Chicago: University of Chicago Press, 2017), 365.

8. Kripal, *Secret Body*, 365.

9. Kripal, *Secret Body*, 366.

10. See Richard Rohr, "Confessions about Panentheism," Deepak Chopra, "Making God Necessary," and the other pieces in Philip Clayton and

Andrew M. Davis, *How I Found God in Everyone and Everywhere: an Anthology of Spiritual Memoirs*, (Rhinebeck: Monkfish Book Publishing Company, 2018.)

11. Gabriella Llewelyn, "The Thin Places." G. Llewellyn, August 17, 2019, www.gabriella-llewellyn.com/the-thin-places.

12. Ernesto de Martino, Primitive Magic: the Psychic Powers of Shamans and Sorcerers, (Cary: Prism, 1990,) 90.

13. In *Psychomagic*, LeValley facilitates relational conversation with Jodorowsky through a series of interviews. In many cases below, Jodorowsky is the generator of the thoughts expressed and LeValley their facilitator and documentarian. I've tried to distinguish this in the citations below.

14. Alejandro Jodorowsky. *Psychomagic: the Transformative Power of Shamanic Psychotherapy*, (Rochester: Inner Traditions, 2010,).

15. De Martino, *Primitive Magic,* 20.

16. Winifred Gallagher, *The Power of Place: How Our Surroundings Shape Our Thoughts, Emotions, and Actions*, (New York: Harper Perennial, 2007,) 89-98.

17. Oliver Burkeman, "This Column Will Change Your Life: Where Heaven and Earth Collide," The Guardian, March 22, 2014, www.theguardian.com/lifeandstyle/2014/mar/22/this-column-change-your-life-heaven-earth

18. Brockman, Norbert, *Encyclopedia of Sacred Places*, (Santa Barbara: ABC-CLIO), vii.

19. David Douglas, *The Atlas of Sacred and Mystical Sites: Discover Places of Mystical Power from around the World*, (London: Godsfield Press, 2007,) 9.

20. Eric Weiner, "Where Heaven and Earth Come Closer," The New York Times, March 11, 2012, www.nytimes.com/2012/03/11/travel/thin-places-where-we-are-jolted-out-of-old-ways-of-seeing-the-world.html.

21. Theresa Bridges, interview with the author, [location], August 16, 2019.

22. JoAnne Marie Terrell, interview by author, online, August 14, 2019.

23. Heiwa no Bushi, interview by author, online, August, 2019

24. Bushi, interview.

25. Bushi, interview.

26. Mike Morrell, interview with the author, online, August 8, 2019.

27. Anita Rao and Grant Holub-Moorman, *The State of Things*, "Bombs, Beavers And Butterfly Biologists: What Fort Bragg Teaches Us About Saving A Species," July 31, 2019, WUNC Chapel Hill. https://www.wunc.org/science-technology/2020-04-01/

bombs-beavers-and-butterfly-biologists-what-fort-bragg-teaches-us-about-saving-a-species

28.	Patricia Hannon, "Corps Cadavres: Heroes and Heroines in the Tales of Perrault," in *The Great Fairy Tale Tradition: from Straparola and Basile to the Brothers Grimm: Texts Criticism*, ed. Jack David Zipes, (New York: W.W. Norton & Company, 2001,) 939, 940, 947.

29.	Bernheimer, Kate, *Horse, Flower, Bird: Stories*, (Minneapolis: Coffee House Press, 2010).

30.	Donald Haase, "Children, War, and the Imaginative Space of Fairy Tales," *The Lion and the Unicorn*, vol. 24, no. 3 (2000): 372. doi:10.1353/uni.2000.0030.

31.	Jack David Zipes, *The Great Fairy Tale Tradition: from Straparola and Basile to the Brothers Grimm: Texts and Criticism*, (New York: W.W. Norton & Company, 2001,) 848.

32.	Jack David Zipes, *Great Fairy Tale Tradition*, 849.

33.	Of course there are a bajillion lovely ways to use your bodies in digital spaces, as so many movement and meditation teachers have taught us during pandemics. Do this.

34.	The Shakespeare Theatre Association's 2023 Conference was hosted by Shakespeare in Paradise and partly held at the Dundas Centre for the Performing Arts in Nassau, Bahamas.

35.	More on DE-CRUIT's impressive work at decruit.org.

36.	Think things like "shame," "lack of belonging," "rage," and so on.

37.	I owe the start of much of this thinking to Dr. Ralph Alan Cohen, a mentor of mine in graduate school at Mary Baldwin College (now University) and the American Shakespeare Center in Staunton, Virginia. I heard Ralph introduce the idea of "ambient attention," where the audience may choose to pay attention to any number of things – play, not play, actors as well as audience, other people, food, sound, spectacle – in a kind of ballpark atmosphere.

WORKS CITED & CONSULTED

Bentley, Jane, and Neil Paynter. *Around a Thin Place: an Iona Pilgrimage Guide*. Glasgow: Wild Goose, 2011. Print.

Bernheimer, Kate. *Horse, Flower, Bird: Stories*. Minneapolis: Coffee House Press, 2010.

Bettelheim, Bruno. "Hansel and Gretel." In *The Classic Fairy Tales*, edited by Maria Tatar, pp. 273–280. New York: W.W. Norton., 1999.

"BodhiChristo." BodhiChristo. December 20, 2022. www.bodhichristo.com.

Brown, Adrienne Maree. *Emergent Strategy: Shaping Change, Changing Worlds*. AK Press, 2021.

Burkeman, Oliver. "This Column Will Change Your Life: Where Heaven and Earth Collide." *The Guardian*, March 22, 2014. www.theguardian.com/lifeandstyle/2014/mar/22/this-column-change-your-life-heaven-earth.

Clayton, Philip, and Andrew M. Davis. *How I Found God in Everyone and Everywhere: an Anthology of Spiritual Memoirs*. Rhinebeck: Monkfish Book Publishing Company, 2018.

Douglas, David. *The Atlas of Sacred and Mystical Sites: Discover Places of Mystical Power from around the World*. London: Godsfield Press, 2007.

DeMuth, Mary E. *Thin Places: a Memoir*. Grand Rapids: Zondervan, 2010.

Gallagher, Winifred. *The Power of Place: How Our Surroundings Shape Our Thoughts, Emotions, and Actions*. New York: Harper Perennial, 2007.

Gungor, Michael, et al. "Buddhist (Part 1)." *The Liturgists Podcast*. Podcast audio. February 7, 2019. theliturgists.com/podcast.

Haase, Donald. "Children, War, and the Imaginative Space of Fairy Tales." *The Lion and the Unicorn*, vol. 24, no. 3 (2000): pp. 360–377. Project MUSE.

Hannon, Patricia. "Corps Cadavres: Heroes and Heroines in the Tales of Perrault." In *The Great Fairy Tale Tradition: from Straparola and Basile to the Brothers Grimm: Texts, Criticism*, edited by Jack David Zipes, pp. 933–957. New York: W.W. Norton & Company, 2001.

Heiwa No Bushi. Interview, online, August 2019.

Hookham, Lama Shenpen. *The Mandala of Sacred Space: Setting up Your Practice at Home (Living the Awakened Heart)*. Scotts Valley: CreateSpace Independent Publishing Platform, 2014.

Jodorowsky, Alejandro. *Psychomagic: The Transformative Power of Shamanic Psychotheraphy*. Rochester: Inner Traditions, 2010.

Kimmerer, Robin Wall. *Braiding Sweetgrass*. Minneapolis: Milkweed Editions, 2013.

Kripal, Jeffrey. *Secret Body: Erotic and Esoteric Currents in the History of Religions*. Chicago: University of Chicago Press, 2017.

Llewelyn, Gabriella. "The Thin Places." *G. Llewellyn*. August 17, 2019. www.gabriella-llewellyn.com/the-thin-places.

Lüthi, Max. *Once upon a Time: on the Nature of Fairy Tales*. Bloomington: Indiana University Press, 1976.

Martino, Ernesto De. *Primitive Magic: the Psychic Powers of Shamans and Sorcerers*. Vancouver: Prism, 1990.

Morrell, Mike. Interview, online, August 8, 2019.

Nutting, Alissa. *Unclean Jobs for Women and Girls*. New York: Ecco, 2018.

Rao, Anita, and Grant Holub-Moorman. "Bombs, Beavers And Butterfly Biologists: What Fort Bragg Teaches Us About Saving A Species." *The State of Things*. WUNC Chapel Hill. Video. July 31, 2019.

Roberts, Mark D. "Thin Places." *Mark D. Roberts*, August 17, 2019. www.patheos.com/blogs/markdroberts/series/thin-places/.

Persinger, Michael A. *Climate, Buildings and Behaviour*. Winnipeg: The Institute of Urban Studies UP, 1988.

---. *Neuropsychological Bases of God Beliefs*. Westport: Praeger, 1987.

"Sacred Places." *Psychology Today*. Sussex Publishers. August 17, 2019. www.psychologytoday.com/us/articles/199301/sacred-places.

Tatar, Maria, and Brothers Grimm. "The Juniper Tree." In *The Classic Fairy Tales: Texts, Criticism*, edited by Maria Tatar, pp. 245–252. New York: W.W. Norton & Company, 2017.

Tatar, Maria. "Introduction: Tricksters." In *The Classic Fairy Tales: Texts, Criticism*, edited by Maria Tatar, pp. 229–235. New York: W.W. Norton & Company, 2017.

Taylor, Daniel. *In Search of Sacred Places*. Jamaica: Bog Walk, 2005.

Terrell, JoAnne Marie. Interview, online, August 14, 2019

"Thomasville Buddhist Center." *Thomasville Buddhist Center*. August 17, 2019. www.tvilledharma.org.

"Unveiling the Thin Places." *Fathom Mag*. January 9, 2017. www.fathommag.com/stories/unveiling-the-thin-places.

Wargo, Eric. "The Night Shirt." *The Night Shirt*. December 20, 2022. www.thenightshirt.com.

Weiner, Eric. "Where Heaven and Earth Come Closer." *The New York Times*, March 9, 2012. www.nytimes.com/2012/03/11/travel/thin-places-where-we-are-jolted-out-of-old-ways-of-seeing-the-world.html.

Wing, Sherin. *Designing Sacred Spaces*. Oxfordshire: Routledge, 2018.

Zipes, Jack David. *The Great Fairy Tale Tradition: from Straparola and Basile to the Brothers Grimm: Texts Criticism*. New York: W.W. Norton & Company, 2001.

Ingram Content Group UK Ltd.
Milton Keynes UK
UKHW021026140323
418548UK00009B/77